Who's Who in EastEnders

WHO'S WHO in EastEnders

by Kate Lock

This book is published to
accompany the BBC Television series
EastEnders

BBC Head of Drama Series: Mal Young

Published by BBC Worldwide, Woodlands,
80 Wood Lane, London W12 oTT

First published 2000
Copyright © BBC Worldwide 2000
Written by Kate Lock

ISBN o 563 55178 X

Editorial Consultant:
Sharon Batten

Commissioning Editor:
Emma Shackleton

Design and editing by TOWN

Cover design by Feref

Picture Researcher:
Miriam Hyman

Map drawn by TOWN

Printed and bound in Great Britain by Butler & Tanner,
Frome and London
Colour Separations by IBA Graphics, London
Cover printed by Belmont Press, Northampton

contents

Introduction by Kate Lock

Fifteen years ago, when *EastEnders* started on 19 February 1985, I was just 24, fresh out of university, and about to embark on a career in journalism. I find it hard to believe it was that long ago when Dirty Den got schoolgirl Michelle Fowler pregnant. I remember them meeting on the towpath so clearly. But that's one of the things I've noted about staying faithful to *EastEnders*: it telescopes time. Researching this book, and my *EastEnders*' novelisations, I was forever muttering, 'It can't be that long since Sharon left/Debs died/Kathy was raped/ Bianca got married.' It always seems like just a couple of years ago. Sometimes it seems like yesterday.

I don't know why this should be.

Perhaps it's because for half an hour three times a week I slip into this parallel life with people who are as familiar – sometimes, regrettably, more familiar – than the far-away family, friends and relatives I only get to see three times a year. And I've known my Albert Square mates a long time now. I know their foibles, their secrets, their dreams. I gossip about them. I know how they'll react. They make me laugh. And cry. And shout rude things. Hell, if that's not a relationship, what is?

Writing the entries for this *Who's Who*, which is a celebration of the main *EastEnders*' characters over the past fifteen years, what worries me more is realising that there are a few characters and events I have no recollection of at all. I won't point

them out – any gaps like that have been ably plugged by *EastEnders*' saintly archivist Sharon Batten, who provided all the research – but I keep wondering: what was happening to me then? Was I taken up by aliens? Permanently drunk? Or did I just have a brilliant social life? (Nah, would've put the video on.) I think I was in Canada. It's the only explanation.

So many characters have passed through Walford since *EastEnders* started that I simply haven't been able to include them all. I trust there are no glaring omissions – those favourites who've been and gone are included under 'Blasts from the past', or, if they are related to a current *EastEnders* family, under 'Significant others', to make them easier to find. Most entries are arranged under families because

that seems the most obvious way to do it – and, I hope, it helps make sense of the tangled web of relationships and marriages that exists in Albert Square!

I love *EastEnders*. I love the fact that the characters are so engaging. I love the fact that it still manages to shock, excite and entertain – even if what shocked back at the start (Colin and Barry's first gay kiss) hardly raises an eyebrow now (Simon and Tony snogged all the time). There are new shocks all the time. Matthew's twisted revenge on Steve Owen is a good example, made all the more effective by the creepy build-up. When it comes to cranking up tension, *EastEnders* excels like no other soap.

The show's more than earned its Baftas for Best Drama Serial and Best Soap (not to mention the host of awards from various TV magazines) and its position at the top of the ratings: eighteen million and more people can't be wrong. *EastEnders,* which was seen as ambitious when it was launched as a bi-weekly drama serial back in 1985, has run thrice-weekly since April 1994 and continues to go from strength to strength. And to move with the times. They may have changed the theme tune (twice); they may have redrawn the map (three times), but even the Dome, symbol of the new Millennium, has been put firmly in its place: as a backdrop for the Mitchell brother's plunge into the Thames – and the Millennium double wedding, of course!

Kate Lock was born in Oxford, where she grew up and began her career as a journalist on the *Oxford Star*. She moved to London, where she worked for *Radio Times* for six years, and continues to write for the magazine as a freelancer. She has written six television drama novelisations: Jimmy McGovern's *The Lakes* (as K.M. Lock) for BBC/Penguin; *Where the Heart is: Home* and *Where the Heart is: Relative Values* (Headline) and *Blood Ties: The Life and Loves of Grant Mitchell, Tiffany's Secret Diary* and *Bianca's Secret Diary* (BBC). She now lives in York with her husband, Stephen, and daughter, Isis.

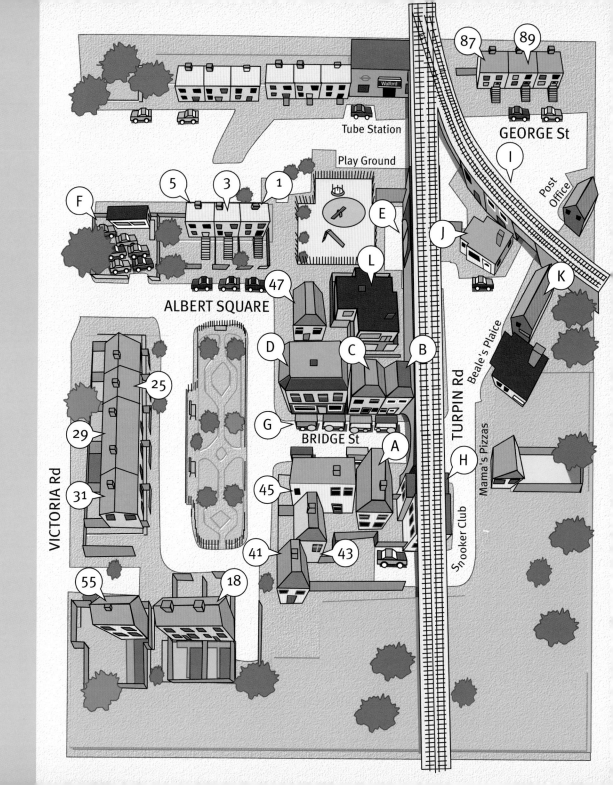

George Street

(87) Irene, Terry

(89) Rosa, Teresa, Nicky, Gianni

(89) **Basement**
Beppe and Little Joe, Nina

Albert Square

Queen Vic
Peggy, Frank, Janine

(1) **Basement**
Doctor's Surgery

(3) **Top**
Mick and Kim

(5) Phil, Jamie, Dan

(18) Bridge House

(25) Robbie (and Wellard), Sonia, Jim, Ricky

(29) Ian, Steven, Peter and Lucy

(31) Melanie, Jeff

(41) Pat and Roy

(43) **Top**
Steve, Jackie

(45) Pauline, Martin, Dot

(47) **Ground**
Barry, Natalie

Victoria Road

(55) Lisa, Mark

Businesses

(A) **Café**
Robbie
(Ian/Phil owners)

(B) **Launderette**
Pauline
Dot
(Owned by
Mr Papadopolous)

(C) **First 'til Last**
Terry
Irene

(D) **Queen Vic**
Peggy
Frank
Dan
Melanie
Nina

(E) **Arches**
Phil
Ricky

(F) **Car Lot**
Roy
Frank

(G) **Market**
Mark – Fruit and Veg
Teresa – Clothes
Mick – CDs
Jamie – Bric-a-brac

(H) **E20**
Steve (owner)
Beppe (owner)
Billy

(I) **Giuseppes**
Rosa
Gianni
Teresa
Jackie

(J) **Beale's Market**
Ian

(K) **Video Shop**
Barry

(L) **Health Club**
Steve (owner)
Phil (owner)

EastEnders Map

the families

Phil and Grant earned themselves the nicknames 'Tweedledum and Tweedledee' when they first came to the Square, but it's easy to tell the bald bruvs apart – Phil's the one with the red face, stubbled chin and paunch who still manages to have beautiful women throw themselves at him. Unfortunately, most threw themselves at Grant, too, because he was better-looking, which has resulted in some spectacular brotherly bust-ups. Phil ended up in intensive care after Grant found out he'd dallied with Sharon (*below*), though their relationship, which somehow survived Sharongate, finally took a dive – into the Thames – after Phil learned that Grant had bedded his ex, Kathy. So much for the Mitchell brothers against the world... Now that hardman Grant's off the scene, cuddly Phil has taken over his bad-boy mantle, taking his bitterness out on his

Phil Mitchell

The one with the red face, stubbled chin and paunch

Born 20.01.61
(Steve McFadden)

nearest and dearest. Peggy and Frank have borne the brunt of this, Peggy for a lifetime of favouring Grant, and Frank for – well, being Frank. To spite the pair of them, Phil flogged his half of the Vic to Dan Sullivan for a fiver and is revelling in the brinkmanship going on behind the bar. While he doesn't have Grant's flammable temperament, Phil's always been happy to lend his fists when occasion demands, having been a debt collector and occasional heavy – and when it doesn't, as Kathy discovered when he became an alcoholic and slung a punch at her. After she decamped to South Africa with their son, Ben, Phil was left shambling around in his overalls like a Teletubby looking for a big hug. The lovely Lisa obliged, but now she's pregnant with his baby, Phil doesn't want to know. Come on, Phil, lighten up. Someone's got to give Peggy a grandchild that doesn't live on another continent...

Mitchell
Jamie

Born 07.11.82

(Jack Ryder)

The Square's heartthrob (he has been described as looking like a cross between David Beckham and Leonardo di Caprio), 17-year-old Jamie has become something of a surrogate son to Phil Mitchell, who rescued his orphaned godson from his violent uncle Billy and took him in. Since then, poor Jamie has also been a surrogate parent to the motherless Courtney (*below*), a surrogate brother to loner Lisa and a surrogate boyfriend to superbitch Janine Butcher, all of which is enough to do anyone's head in, let alone a kid with Jamie's artistic temperament. His preferred way of working his emotions out is with a can of spray paint, for which he shows great talent – he was clearly wasted working in Beale's Market and has great potential as an interior designer (although his graffiti-covered revamp of E20 wasn't quite what Annie Palmer had in mind). Having been sexually scorned by Janine, to whom he lost his virginity, he is wary of relationships with girls and prefers to play cupid with Phil and Lisa instead. For someone so young and gorgeous this seems a crime, but with looks like Jamie's it can only be a matter of time before he finds himself a nice girl – or Irene Hills takes him as toyboy number two...

His preferred way of working his emotions out is with a can of spray paint

Billy Mitchell

Born 10.05.59

(Perry Fenwick)

Scrawny, wild-haired runt of a man who's a catalyst for trouble – guns, explosions, psychopathic loan sharks, murderous drug dealers, that sort of thing. He's the younger brother (along with Jamie's dad, Charlie) of Peggy's late husband, Eric, though none of the other Mitchells likes to think of him as 'fam'ly', particularly Jamie, who was brought up by him after his dad died. Since Billy's idea of parenting was to get drunk and beat him up, Jamie goes into graffiti overdrive every time Billy descends on Walford, bringing out Phil's thuggish fatherly instincts. Billy is held in great contempt by the Mitchell bruvs, who regard him as a lower lifeform than a worm, although that didn't stop Grant approaching him for dosh to buy the snooker hall, triggering a chain of events that led to his and Phil's disastrous dip in the river. Having crawled back into his hole after that debacle, Billy has resurfaced again and has miraculously wangled a job at E20. This is Steve Owen's way of winding Phil up, a move that, with Jamie already quaking in his boots, is bound to end with someone's teeth being kicked in. After all, it's what Mitchell men do best...

Billy is held in great contempt by the Mitchell bruvs who regard him as a lower lifeform than a worm

Significant others
Sam Mitchell

Born 13.05.75

(Danniella Westbrook)

More EastEnd moll than Barbie doll

Headstrong, streetwise and pretty, Phil and Grant's baby sister Sam is a chip off the old Mitchell block, though her methods of manipulation are marginally more subtle than the boys. One bat of a sooty eyelash is enough to charm most men into submission and she can wind doting mum Peggy round her little finger. A late and unplanned addition to the Mitchell family, Sam lost her father when she was ten and is generally on the receiving end of her brothers' heavy-handed paternalism. No man is ever good enough for their little sis, which is strange when you consider that Sam herself hasn't been that choosy – she eloped with thicky Ricky (*above*), mooned around after playboy Clive, slept with David Wicks and took off for the Costas with Guillermo, a Spaniard she barely knew. As for protecting her virtue, the lads are way behind sultry Sam. She's been photographed topless, worked as a 'hostess' in a dubious nightclub and then majored in 'glamour' modelling after an interlude of respectability as a holiday rep. The last time she returned to the Square, Sam, 24, had lost her kittenish cuteness and hardened up, becoming more EastEnd moll than Barbie doll. She endeared herself to Beppe di Marco despite being drunk and throwing up, and for a while it seemed as if love might conquer even the Mitchell/di Marco divide. But it was not to be. Beppe dumped her (in the Natural History Museum – though Ancient History might have been more appropriate) and after 'accidentally' sleeping with Steve Owen, Sam realised she'd shot all her bolts and left Walford. Again.

M ad, bad and dangerous to know, that was Grant. And how we loved him for it. After being one of the central characters in *EastEnders* for nine years, his departure in October 1999 marked a turning point. No more the sight of Grant's flaring nostrils and bulging eyes, his indecently short shorts and rippling biceps, for the Square's unlikely lothario has taken off for South America with daughter Courtney, fleeing a coterie of criminals and the rage of brother Phil. The bruvs – Grant, 37, is the younger by a year – had always appeared joined at the jeans pocket, but the curtain came down on their double act after he admitted sleeping with Kathy. Whether it was love or lust, even Grant himself never seemed to

Grant Mitchell

Born 08.07.62
(Ross Kemp)

A woman's place was on a pedestal as far as Grant was concerned, and whenever things went wrong he came over all caveman

know. He thought first wife Sharon was the Real Thing, but then so was Lorraine, and Louise, and even, belatedly, second wife Tiffany. A woman's place was on a pedestal as far as Grant was concerned, and whenever things went wrong he came over all caveman. But then Grant never knew when to stop – an ex-Para, he was trained to kill and, indeed, almost committed murder twice (publican Eddie Royle and Phil) as well as being imprisoned for assaulting a police officer. Grant was a man who never did things by halves: he loved and hated with his entire being (remember his silent scream in the rain?) and it was this machismo, fuelled by his emotional vulnerability, that made him such a compelling character.

Fate and the festive
ratings dealt Tiffany a
double whammy

Tiffany & Courtney Mitchell

Born 13.09.76 **Died** Jan 99
(Martine McCutcheon)

Born 12.03.97
(Josephine & Carissa O'Meara)

Tarty Tiffany was merely a mouthy barmaid at the Vic before she slept with the boss and ended up becoming the second Mrs Grant Mitchell. The fruit of this union, tug-of-love baby Courtney, was what kept this unlikely couple together (once parentage had been proved – Tony Hills was a candidate too), but although Tiffany was always running to best friend Bianca with tales of Grant's excesses, she genuinely loved him. This was more than could be said of Grant, who suffered her as the mother of his much-longed-for child but had little respect for her as a person. Tiff always knew she was second-best but stuck to her guns, seeing off competition in the form of lissom Lorraine, going back to Grant when he hit her and even turning down the chance to sleep with the gorgeous Beppe di Marco. Grant and Tiffany did, finally, get it together and enjoy one perfect moment, but, as is the way with soaps, it was to be the only one. Returning to the Vic glowing with love, Tiffany discovered that Grant had been cheating on her with Louise, her own mother – the ultimate betrayal. She tried to flee Walford with Beppe and Courtney, but fate and the festive ratings dealt her a double whammy: she fell down the stairs and went into a coma, recovering just in time to be run over by Frank Butcher on New Year's Day 1999 (thus going one better than Sharon by departing in a black hearse).

Courtney, Tiffany and Grant's three-year-old daughter, is currently on the run with her daddy in Rio. She was pushed from pillar to post by her warring parents when Tiffany was alive – it was Grant trying to snatch Courtney that lead to Tiff's fatal accident (*opposite*) – while her subsequent upbringing by Grant, Phil and Jamie resembled *Three Men and a Little Lady*. She never said much beyond (tragically) 'Mummy', but now she is presumably speaking Spanish like a native.

Mitchell **Sharon**

Born 22.10.69
(Letitia Dean)

A buxom femme fatale

Sharon was the adopted daughter of Den and Angie Watts, the Vic's original licensees. She grew up, squeezed herself into power suits and became a buxom femme fatale, although the love of her life was never drippy Duncan, wandering Wicksy, growling Grant – whom she married – or Phil, who she had a fling with, but the pub. Her most enduring friendship was with Michelle Fowler, who loved her like a sister, defended her like a Rottweiler and slept with both the men Sharon had been closest to (her father, her ex-husband). When Sharon's stormy relationship with Grant ended in public humiliation (the famous scene when he played her taped 'confession' about Phil to a crowded Vic), he made her life unbearable and demanded a divorce. Sharon fled to her mum in Florida, returning a few months later to get her own back. Soon Grant was following her around like a lovesick puppy but when it came to the crunch, Sharon was too soft to stick the boot in and departed Walford for ever in the time-honoured tradition – a black cab.

Kathy Mitchell

Born 11.05.50

(Gillian Taylforth)

hen *EastEnders* first started, Kathy – or 'Kaff' as she's known throughout the Square – aspired to nothing more ambitious than being Mrs Pete Beale and flogging woolly jumpers. By the time of her last appearance, 15 years later, she had acquired near-goddess status, only slightly tarnished by having spawned son of Satan, Ian Beale (*left*). Alex the vicar, with whom she'd got passionate in the pews, was even prepared to give up the Church for her, while Phil and Grant both thought she was the bestest, purest thing since saintly Sharon and almost committed fratricide over her. Husky-voiced Kathy endured soaps' slings and arrows with dignity and much defiant tossing of her blonde hair. She was raped by Dagmar owner James Willmott-Brown, lost Donna, the daughter she gave away as a teenager, to a drugs overdose, and was hit and humiliated by an alcoholic Phil. Grant wanted to run away with her, but despite succumbing to his manly charms, she has ultimately resisted both Mitchell men and wisely made a new life for herself and son Ben in sunny South Africa.

Husky-voiced Kathy endured soaps' slings and arrows with dignity

Ben Mitchell

Born 21.03.96

(various actors)

hil and Kathy's son had a traumatic start in life when he developed meningitis and nearly died. It left him slightly deaf but otherwise unscathed, and he is maturing nicely – unlike Phil, who was so jealous of Ben as a baby that he too started swigging from a bottle, chucking up, throwing tantrums and flailing his fists. Ben and Phil now have a long-distance relationship, communicating largely by airmail, so the chances of Ben developing normally are probably better than most.

SEE ALSO:
Peggy Butcher (aka Mitchell)

At 64 the old charmer's still capable of sweeping women off their feet

Frank 'Hello Babe' Butcher may be full of bluff and bluster, but at 64 the old charmer's still capable of sweeping women off their feet – well, Peggy anyway – which resulted in some ground-breaking wrinkly snogging pre-watershed. Their union sees Frank back in his natural habitat, exchanging cockney wit and wisdom behind the bar of the Queen Vic (he first ran the pub ten years ago with Pat). This time, though, he's having to share it with 'Desperate' Dan Sullivan, who, aided and abetted by a vindictive Phil, is making life difficult and retirement impossible. Still, Frank's a survivor – he's had to be. He's come back from financial ruin and a complete nervous breakdown, not to mention losing Pat to rival Roy. He also has two deaths on his conscience, most famously Tiffany's, as well as a vagrant who died in the car lot fire (torched by Phil on Frank's say-so to claim the insurance). Frank is father to four children – Clare, Diane, Ricky and the awful Janine, all from his first marriage, though he was never faithful to wife June and when she died he married Pat, who he'd been sleeping with on the QT all along. Pat was the big love of his life and they still manage the odd bonk, generally before one of them remarries, though these days the old love-hound only has eyes for his darlin' Peggy.

The diminutive licensee of the Queen Vic may have changed her surname, but she's got Mitchell stamped through her like a stick of seaside rock. Her obsession with 'Fam'ly' borders on the Mafioso, and her dearest wish is to have all the Mitchells sitting round the dinner table at Christmas, though you'd think by now she'd have learned that this always ends in tears. Still, no matter what scrapes her kids get into (attempted murder, arson, adultery, fraud, upsetting Underworld bosses, to name a few) she generally sticks by them, preferring to mete out her own discipline – a verbal tirade and a stinging slap – rather than involve the Old Bill. She probably gets her right

hook from first husband Eric, a boxer, although he never made the grade professionally and descended into gambling instead. Eric died of cancer and Peggy resumed an affair she'd been having with Kevin, the owner of the local minicab firm, but the relationship turned sour and she moved to Walford to sort her children out instead. She was courted by smoothie George Palmer and would have married him if his criminal connections had not come to light. In the end, it was Frank Butcher who won her heart, leading to some

Her dearest wish is to have all the Mitchells sitting round the dinner table at Christmas

Frank & Peggy Butcher

Born 1936
(Mike Reid)

Born 21.03.42
(Barbara Windsor)

entertaining cat fights with Pat and a 'will-she, won't-she?' moment in church before Peggy turned up, utterly radiant, and made a (fairly) honest man of him. Peggy has always traded on her glamorous appearance and the discovery that she had breast cancer initially devastated her. She squared up to it with typical stoicism and is now finally trying to put her own needs first – if her disaster-prone family will ever let her.

in flagrante with naughty Natalie, and he did go all slushy over first wife Sam Mitchell when he was supposed to be marrying B, but since their wedding he's proved to be a loyal husband and a doting dad to baby Liam. Ricky's well-meaning but easily led – he got a Community Service order for handling Phil's dodgy motors and he went Christmas-tree rustling with Teresa di Marco (who made a play for him herself), incurring Bianca's wrath. Provoking Bianca was something Ricky excelled at, but they had their moments and were brought very close by the death of their first child, Natasha. In the end, though, his dog-like devotion was never enough for B and when he found out about her affair with Dan, even thicky Ricky could read the writing on the wall.

Ricky Butcher

Born 21.02.73
(Sid Owen)

Hapless Ricky has always been a figure of fun. He's a bit of a duffer, completely lacking in tact and rarely opens his mouth without putting his foot in it – which makes his recent transformation (being a posh bird's bit of rough has given him a renewed zest for life) all the more remarkable. Perhaps there's more beneath those greasy mechanic's overalls than meets the eye – certainly the Vic's female regulars swooned over photos of him in his speedway leathers – although it wasn't enough to keep wife Bianca satisfied. Not that much did. She doused Ricky in beer, covered him in chips and set light to his clothes in the street. True, she caught him

Janine Butcher

Born 18.10.83

(Charlie Brooks)

'Vicious', 'manipulative', 'a right little cow'. Janine Butcher has gained quite a lot of names for herself – and she's still only 16. Everyone knew Janine was trouble from the moment Frank married Pat and produced his youngest daughter as the booby prize. As a 6-year-old (*right*) she made Pat's life hell on wheels, running away, screaming, telling tales and throwing tantrums, and she's stuck to the same tactics ever since. Frank, guilty at having been such an inadequate father to her, has developed a blind spot where his little princess's bad behaviour is concerned, and she's now completely out of control. Her behaviour since she turned up recently, having run away from home (she was living in Manchester with big sister Clare), has been pretty much par for the course, although now she's older, Janine does more damage. So far she's got drunk and almost drowned, faked a pregnancy, thrown a wild party and screwed up poor Jamie Mitchell (*above*) even further by enticing him into bed and then broadcasting his lack of prowess to her friends. Uncannily, she looks like a younger version of the much-missed Tiffany, but without her sweetness and sense of humour. Maybe there is a nice person inside Janine's heavily reinforced shell – but then that would make her less interesting to watch.

L anky, lippy Bianca, the Girl with the Gob, could turn the blood in a man's veins to ice with her menacing cry of 'Rick-kay!'. The eldest daughter of Carol Jackson, she caused trouble as soon as she came to the Square by stalking market inspector Tricky Dicky. The freckle-faced firebrand then set her sights on David Wicks, unaware that he was her father, and when he knocked her back she sunk her claws into poor defenceless Ricky Butcher. From then on, the lad was a gonner. Bianca never really loved him and frequently denounced him as 'boring', but he was a steady bet and, after rashly sleeping with Lenny Wallace, B realised she had a good thing going with Ricky and married him. She had her share of sadness, losing a baby to spina bifida, but a second child, Liam, was born healthy. For a clothes-stall owner Bianca had a bizarre

Bianca Butcher

Born 17.07.77
(Patsy Palmer)

sense of style, but it all became clear at her interview for a fashion design course when she named Vivienne Westwood as her influence. She was a loyal friend, especially to Tiffany, and a tenacious foe, as both Natalie and Louise found to their cost. When she finally fell from grace herself by having an affair with Dan, her mother's intended, there were few in Albert Square who had any sympathy for the razor-tongued redhead. The fling fizzled out acrimoniously, Carol aborted Dan's baby, and a tear-stained Bianca boarded a train for Manchester with little Liam, a heavy suitcase and an even heavier conscience.

There were few in Albert Square who had any sympathy for the razor-tongued redhead

Butcher
Liam

Born 25.12.98
(Jack & Tom Godolphin)

The first shock for baby Liam, arriving four weeks early into the world on Christmas Day 1999, was seeing Grant Mitchell's ugly mug. Bianca's *bête noir* was forced to help deliver her baby when she went into labour in the Vic and, given the fact that they were at daggers drawn over his treatment of Tiffany, even B had to admit Grant did a good job. Since then, however, Liam has largely remained bundled up in his buggy, becoming a tug-of-love child in true *EastEnders* tradition after Ricky found out about his wife's infidelity and gave her the boot. After being advised that he was unlikely to get custody, Ricky reluctantly let Bianca take Liam with her to Manchester, where the little lad is now living it up in the college crèche.

Butcher
Diane

Born 04.01.74

(Sophie Lawrence)

Frank's middle daughter, Diane, has always been sensitive and artistic – she once painted an outsize mural on the side of the B&B – so it's no surprise she's now living a Bohemian existence in a Parisian squat. As a 16-year-old she ran away from home and lived rough for three months, becoming involved with a manipulative middle-aged photographer who took nude photos of her and subsequently exhibited a naked statue – recognisably Diane – in the middle of the Square! She had a schoolgirl crush on builder Paul Priestly but Mark Fowler was her first big love and, having faced up to his HIV status together, they have retained a strong friendship. The move

to France came about in 1991 when Diane went on holiday there – and never came back. She has a young son, Jacques (*far left*), who she dumped on Bianca and Ricky to follow her Cameroonian musician boyfriend on tour. The mischievous French boy gave Ricky the runaround – leading a pregnant Bianca to think he didn't want kids and almost go through with an abortion – but his errant mum eventually reclaimed him and returned to Paris to read her Simone de Beauvoir novels in splendid squalor.

It's no surprise she's now living a Bohemian existence in a Parisian squat

Aunt Sal

Born 1940
(Anna Karen)

Aunt Sal

Mo Butcher

Born 1921 **Died** Dec 92
(Edna Dore)

Frank's mother Mo was a fearsome old battleaxe who assumed a matriarchal role in the Queen Vic as if to the manor born, only her manor was Walthamstow. Pat's nose was put severely out of joint by her mother-in-law's interfering and an intimidated Frank got caught in the crossfire, but Mo was indomitable – or seemed to be. She ruled the roost at the B&B (one of Pat and Frank's other businesses), bullied council bosses about the community centre and became a beady-eyed Brown Owl, although she was eventually sacked from the Brownies for lying about her age. Then things started to go wrong: she became increasingly forgetful, flooded the B&B and set fire to her house in a painfully true-to-life portrayal of the onset of Alzheimer's Disease. As she deteriorated further, Frank, unable to give his old mum the round-the-clock care she now needed, sent for his sister Joan, who looked after Mo 'til she died on New Year's Eve 1992.

Peggy's blabbermouth sister, who she usually disappears off to visit in times of crisis, remains largely an unseen presence. She has made an appearance a couple of times, once to stand in for Peggy at Grant and Tiffany's Blessing, when she tried to take over the proceedings, and once to take refuge in the Vic after her husband Harold ran off with a dolly bird. She has a hide thicker than Peggy's, a penchant for interfering and a tendency to become loud and hideously embarrassing after a couple of drinks, winning hen-pecked Harold the sympathy vote.

SEE ALSO:
Pat Evans (aka Butcher)

Think Pauline Fowler and the words 'beige' and 'cardigan' spring to mind. Or they used to. After 15 years of dowdy knitwear, having a new man in her life – Jeff Healy – has given Pauline's wardrobe an unexpected boost. It's certainly time long-suffering Pauline let her hair down. She's always had a Blitz mentality, soldiering on while her children dropped various bombshells on her: running away, imprisonment,

Pauline Fowler

Born 11.03.45

(Wendy Richard)

Marriage to 'My Arthur' – who was as woolly as one of her cardies – was never exactly a bundle of fun

drugs, HIV (Mark), illegitimate children, unsuitable men (Michelle), juvenile delinquency (Martin). On top of which, marriage to 'My Arthur' – who was as woolly as one of her cardies – was never exactly a bundle of fun. Pauline stood by him after he ended up behind bars, not once but twice – although he was set up the second time by creepy Willy Roper, who even had the front to make a play for her while Arthur was inside (he got to Jersey – the island, not the jumper – but no further). And then there was Arthur's affair with brazen Mrs Hewitt, while Pauline, who had been offered the chance to trip the light fantastic with bespangled crooner Danny Taurus, had stayed loyal. She's always been old-fashioned, just like her mother, Lou Beale, seeing it as her duty to keep the family going, especially since the death of her twin brother, Pete (Beale), and, latterly, Arthur. Then there's her other important function – keeping the Square's dirty washing circulating at the launderette, with the help of colleague and housemate Dot Cotton. Without their talent for speculation and gossip over the service washes, *EastEnders* wouldn't be a true 'soap', now would it?

Fowler
Mark

Born 02.02.68

(Todd Carty)

Mark Fowler has lived with being HIV+ for a decade and has looked so well for most of this time that his recent collapse and near-death from pneumonia was a shock to everyone – including him. Mark's thought to have contracted the virus from Gill, a girl he lived with during his wanderlust years, although this was never proven. (Staid Mark was actually a rebellious youth. He ran away from home at 17, got involved with drugs, was banged up in a detention centre for burglary and didn't return to live in the Square until he was 22.) Mark and Gill were eventually reunited, but by then she had developed full-blown Aids. He married her on 23 June 1992 and she died the next day. Sadly, Mark's never had much joy with relationships: he proposed to Diane Butcher, but she disappeared off to France; drippy Shelley was too clingy; lecturer Rachel Kominski blew hot and cold, and although it seemed as if he and sensible Scots girl Ruth were made for each other, their marriage fell apart when she was distracted by Conor Flaherty's smiling Irish eyes. Since then Mark, who owns the Beale family fruit-and-veg stall, has been going it alone, struggling with an exhausting drug regime – which he misguidedly stopped taking, triggering his collapse – and harbouring a secret love for market inspector Lisa *(left)*. Unable to stand Phil's cavalier treatment of his pregnant lodger, he confessed his true feelings, but was left feeling a lemon when she told him she only liked him as a friend.

Mark's never had much joy with relationships

Martin Fowler

Born 30.07.85

(James Alexandrou)

M artin's still only 14, but he's already got himself into more trouble than most people do in a lifetime. He's become so obnoxious that Harry Enfield's creation, Kevin the Teenager, looks positively convivial by comparison. His conception was an accident – Pauline was 40 when she had him after defying Lou's instructions to have an abortion – and what with the distraction of Mark and Michelle's antics, Martin's always come a poor third among the Fowler children. Unsurprisingly, perhaps, Martin's always been rather surly; this has worsened since the death of his father and grunting has now become his main form of communication. Elder brother Mark tried, and failed, to get through to him by talking about football, although they've grown closer since Mark's brush with death. Pauline's new bloke Jeff is having the most success – Martin has been known to utter whole sentences recently – and has even got him interested in handyman work. Cynics might argue that Martin's glimmer of enthusiasm is just so that he can learn useful techniques for breaking and entering: a latter-day Artful Dodger (but without the charm), he has already been cautioned for theft and got away with a lot more. Currently he's become more interested in scoring with girls, specifically Nicky di Marco. Give him four years and he'll be giving Grant Mitchell's record some serious competition.

A latter-day Artful Dodger (but without the charm)

Poor old Arthur. He wore a permanently bemused expression, as if he was never quite up to speed with life, and that was pretty much the case. He was an innocent man, good-hearted – and very gullible. He only proposed to Pauline because he felt sorry for her (she had 'flu and he wanted to cheer her up). That led to 31 years of marriage, three kids and a great deal of trouble and strife. Unemployed Arthur wanted to give daughter

Fowler
Arthur

Born 19.08.43 **Died** May 96

(Bill Treacher)

He was an innocent man good-hearted – and very gullible

Michelle a decent wedding, but 'borrowing' the Christmas Club money cost him 28 days in clink – and a nervous breakdown. Another attempt to make money/find work saw him unwittingly involved in an illegal racket with the Mitchells, delivering forged MOT certificates, for which Michelle made Phil take the rap. He even set himself up as a gardener, but ended up sowing more than nasturtiums with tenacious divorcee Christine Hewitt (the so-called 'Bonk of the Year'). Most tragic of all, when Arthur did eventually find fulfilment, working for the 'flowering wilderness' campaign, he was duped into putting his signature on what turned out to be his own death warrant. Sent down for embezzlement – while it was Willy Roper mopping up the cash – Arthur's spirit broke. He was injured in prison and died shortly after his release, whilst digging his beloved allotment.

Her first whopping mistake was to lose her virginity at 16 to 'Dirty' Den Watts

Michelle Fowler

Born 30.07.69

(Susan Tully)

Dogged, dour and argumentative, Michelle always acted as if she held the moral high ground, but her toughness was a front. True, she could fight her corner – witness her bravery when Dougie Briggs lay siege to the Vic and she got shot – but underneath her prickly exterior Michelle just wanted to be loved. The trouble was, she had an absolute genius for picking the wrong guys. Her first whopping mistake was to lose her virginity at 16 to 'Dirty' Den Watts *(left)*. Little Vicki was born nine months later. Pauline *(above)* sussed who the father was, but no-one else did and Michelle kept her secret until after Den's death, when the revelation caused a major rift between her and best friend Sharon. No man could ever match Den in her eyes, and she jilted Lofty *(above, far right)* at the altar, although she later married him in a discreet registry office ceremony. Even so, Michelle was never content and subsequently aborted his baby, devastating poor Lofty, who left. After that there was a succession of blokes: Danny, the married computer salesman; Clyde, who she ended up going on the run with; student wacko Jacko; Geoff, a sports-jacketed university lecturer; Gary, from the council's housing department, and

Grant. Yes, Grant. Michelle's sworn enemy – she stood shoulder-to-shoulder with Sharon against him – did the deed with her in the Vic after an evening of hurling abuse at each other, and hey presto – another pregnancy. Unable to face being linked with him, she got a research job and moved to America, where she gave birth to Mark Jnr in May 1996. To this day, Grant remains none the wiser.

Ruth Fowler

Born 20.08.66

(Caroline Paterson)

Ruth could be as abrasive as her harsh Scottish accent, which didn't endear her to everybody, but one thing people did agree on was how good she was for Mark. They met at a hospice, where they were both visiting friends dying of Aids, and the experience gave them an emotional shortcut to a relationship. Ruth was the daughter of a strict Presbyterian minister, who refused to give his blessing to her union with Mark and disowned her when she married him anyway. A nursery worker, Ruth persuaded herself – and Mark – that she was happy about not having kids, but it became obvious that she was fooling herself. They tried fostering a 6-year-old called Jessie, but having to give her back proved too heart-breaking to go through again. By this time, the rot had set in on their marriage, which had been beset by money worries and trust issues after Mark lost a fortune gambling. When feckless Irishman Conor Flaherty started sniffing around Ruth, Mark became insanely jealous and the relationship fell apart. After they'd split, Ruth succumbed to Conor's charm and got pregnant. It was an accident, but she had her long-awaited baby at last. She left Walford contemplating a future as a single mother – as her close friend Gita had done at one point – but Conor belatedly faced up to his responsibilities and went after her.

One thing people did agree on was how good she was for Mark

Vicki Fowler

Born 27.05.86
(Samantha Leigh Martin)

It's a shock to think that little Vicki is now a 13-year-old high-school girl in America. She's probably got braces and ambitions to be a cheer leader, although it's not the sort of thing mum Michelle would approve of. When we last saw Vicki she was still a pixie-like tot, apparently oblivious to all the hoo-haa about her daddy, Den, ending up dead in the canal and unfazed by 'Auntie' Sharon confessing to being her half-sister. Mind you, Vicki had a few dramas of her own. She developed meningitis (as *EastEnders* tots tend to do – see also Ben Mitchell) and was later abducted (as *EastEnders* tots tend to be – see also Billy Jackson), giving Michelle a frightening few days until the childless woman who had taken her was tracked down. Now she has an American step-father and a younger brother, Mark. So who cares if none of them are related?

Gill Fowler

Born 1963 **Died** Jun 92
(Susanna Dawson)

Tragic Gill only bore the Fowler name for a day before she died of Aids at the age of 28. She had lived with Mark in Newcastle and they had been happy together, but after discovering she was HIV+ she couldn't handle the implications and ran away to London without telling him. Mark tried to find her, without success, but she eventually traced him to Walford, where she plucked up courage to tell him the truth. They made their peace, but by then she had contracted full-blown Aids and soon after was taken into a hospice. Mark and Gill married a few months later in a moving ceremony (*above, with Michelle and Rachel in attendance*) that touched all who saw it.

Once upon a time, Ian Beale was a nice boy. A bit wimpy, perhaps, not what you'd call a man's man, but he was caring and pleasant and spoke politely to people. Recognise the description? No? Surely it can't be the Hitler-Hague hybrid we know and hate? The fish-and-chip magnate trying to turn Walford into the capital of Capitalism? The man whose first wife was so desperate to be rid of him that she hired a hitman? The man so desperate to net a new wife he pretended his own daughter was dying? Yup, that's the one.

Ian Beale

An obsessive, obnoxious money-monster

Born 01.03.69

(Adam Woodyatt)

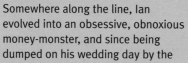

Somewhere along the line, Ian evolved into an obsessive, obnoxious money-monster, and since being dumped on his wedding day by the gorgeous Mel (*above right*) he's become twice as twisted. But then Ian's never had much luck with blondes: Sharon Watts chucked him and Cindy (*left*) walked out on him twice. At one point, the bloke was reduced to kerb-crawling. Feel sorry for him? Don't. Ian's always pretended to be magnanimous, doing things for the community (the residents association, standing for the council, throwing street parties) but it's inspired by self-interest. He has undermined the market with his cheapo shop, had half the Square in hock to him as a loan-shark, stitched innocent people up and even tried to con his own mother (over the sale of the café). His one redeeming feature is his devotion to his children, Steven, Peter and Lucy. We know Ian's human – we've seen him bleed – so let's hope someone gets through to him before his heart sets in stone.

Lucy & Peter Beale

Born 09.12.93
(Casey Anne Rothery)

Born 09.12.93
(Joseph Shade)

Six-year-old twins, Lucy (*above, centre*) and Peter (*above, far right*) are the result of Ian and Cindy's reconciliation. And yes, this time Ian is their father (although Tricky Dicky was a frontrunner for a time). The twins endured a dramatic separation after Cindy snatched Steven and Peter but didn't manage to get Lucy in time. Ian, desperate to protect his one remaining child, holed up in the house with her and lived like a recluse until Pat talked some sense into him. Since Cindy's death, Lucy, like all the Beale children, has been missing a mother figure and latched onto Mel. When Lucy fell ill a few months ago with suspected non-Hodgkin's Lymphoma she was admitted to hospital for tests, sending Ian's stress levels off the scale. Mel, floored by the possibility that Lucy's illness was terminal, couldn't bring herself to call off the wedding. Ian realised this was all that was keeping her with him and, when Lucy received the all-clear, lied to Mel that his daughter's days were numbered. Lucy got to wear her bridesmaid's dress, and very pretty she looked in it too, but there was no longed-for new mummy when Mel discovered the truth.

Steven Beale

Born 26.12.89
(Edward Savage)

Steven has experienced much acrimony and sadness in his life, with the result that he's much more mature than his 10 years. Steven is Ian's eldest child, although he's not actually Ian's, but Wicksy's. Ian only discovered this some months after he married Cindy and went berserk, crashing his van deliberately. On his release from hospital, he tracked Cindy, Wicksy and babe-in-arms Steven down to Devon and surprised them brandishing a shotgun. That pretty much set the tone for Steven's childhood. When Cindy and Ian were reunited two years later, things went downhill again and she ended up fleeing with Steven and brother Peter to Italy. Having got used to eating pasta that wasn't shaped like Postman Pat, the children were kidnapped back by the Mitchells and then became the objects of a bitter custody wrangle. Cindy ended up in prison for Ian's shooting and subsequently died in childbirth. Her death affected Steven much more than the other two children and he went to her funeral in Devon. He's a responsible, sensitive boy who often looks out for his younger brother and sister because daddy is too distracted by empire-building. Let's hope the new nanny brings some magic back into his life. Steven needs it.

Pete Beale

Born 11.03.45 **Died** Dec 93

(Peter Dean)

Pete (*below*) was a simple, amiable sort of chap. He wore a big, doggy grin, sold bananas and Brussels sprouts and left others to get on with the complicated things in life. Complications didn't suit Pete. They were beyond his grasp. They got him all stirred up with emotions he couldn't articulate, making him do silly things like drink-driving and hitting policemen. Nice-but-dim Pete was taken for a real ride by his first wife, Pat, who even had a fling with his brother, Kenny (as well as Brian Wicks, Den Watts and most of the other consenting males in Walford). They had two sons, David and Simon, but when Pete found out that Simon wasn't his, he went ballistic and was at one point suspected of being the so-called 'Walford Attacker' after Pat was discovered badly beaten. He divorced Pat in 1965 and married Kathy Hills three years later, fathering the evil Ian. (Pete wasn't keen on Ian doing nancy things like cooking, making him take up boxing instead, which might go some way to explaining his son's behaviour.) Marriage to Kathy wasn't that successful, either – Pete could never get his head round Kathy being raped by Willmott-Brown, thinking that somehow she must have asked for it. Unsurprisingly, Kathy left him and started going out with rival fruit-and-veg man Laurie, making Pete all insecure about the size of his spuds.

He did find happiness in the end, but it was, sadly, short-lived. Rose Chapman was married to the local mobster, who didn't take kindly to his wife absconding with Pete and got his family to rub them out by 'arranging' a car accident. A true East-ending.

Kenny & Lou Beale

Born 1940

(Michael Attwell)

Born 1915 **Died** Jul 88

(Anna Wing)

Pete and Pauline's older brother, Kenny (*above*), did what they never dared to do: escape from Walford. Actually, Kenny's leaving wasn't entirely voluntary (although he was glad of the excuse) – Lou banished him when she got wind of his dalliance with Pat. Deciding to put as much distance between him and the rest of the Beales as possible, he legged it to New Zealand, married and set himself up as a swimming-pool salesman. Kenny's presence has generally been implied rather than seen, although he did appear on screen in 1988, when he and daughter Elizabeth came to visit, triggering a showdown between him, Pete and Pat over Wicksy's parentage (as it turned out, Pat was stringing them both along). Pete went to stay with him for a short while and had a holiday romance with a woman called Barbara. She followed him back to Walford but became homesick and returned. Then, in 1992, Pauline flew out to New Zealand for several months after Kenny had a car crash, coming back determined that she and Arthur should emigrate. Unsurprisingly, Arthur, who'd been bonding with Mrs Hewitt in Pauline's absence, was not impressed with the idea.

Lou Beale (*left*) represented Walford's old days, a time before all the Johnny-Come-Lately's moved to the Square, a time when long-established families like the Fowlers and the Beales held sway and grudges lasted a lifetime. The old matriarch was born in 1915 and lived at 45 Albert Square from the Second World War onwards, renting it from the council. Her husband, Albert, ran the fruit and veg stall, and his father before him, making grandson Mark the fourth generation to work it. Lou was a terrifying old lady with a vicious streak who lived with Arthur and Pauline and dominated their lives until her death from heart disease in 1988. She didn't so much converse as issue edicts, chins wobbling. Family members used to receive summonses,

most memorably from her deathbed, when she called them all in one by one for her parting comments. Few dared deviate from her judgements, although Pauline went against her by refusing to have an abortion and Pat Wicks (Pete's first wife) stood up to her over the row about Wicksy's parentage. Of her children, Pete and Pauline remained in Walford while Kenny went to New Zealand. The other two, Ronnie and Maureen, had both died. But Lou had a secret, which Pauline only discovered many years later – her first child by Albert was conceived out of wedlock and was given up for adoption (becoming Maggie Flaherty). The arch moralist herself had feet of clay, after all.

Cindy Beale

She lied schemed, flirted and flaunted

Born 10.05.68 **Died** Nov 98

(Michelle Collins)

Cindy was a real brazen hussy. She lied, schemed, flirted and flaunted to get what she wanted, and was very successful at it. Despite – or perhaps because of – Cindy's deviousness, she was an immensely popular character. Snatching her kids may have been wrong, but it was Cindy most viewers where rooting for in the dash for the Eurostar train. Scheming Cindy was always a bit of a money-grabber, hence the initial attraction to Ian Beale (*below*), but she really only made a play for him to make wandering Wicksy jealous. Cindy never loved Ian; she married him out of expediency (she was pregnant with Steven), dropped him to go off with Wicksy and then got back together with him three years later because she was alone, broke and miserable as a single mum. It wasn't long before she was up to her old tricks again, lusting after a lifeguard at the swimming pool before she began another affair, this time with David, Wicks brother number two (*above*). Encouraged by his empty promises, she vowed to get shot of Ian and did just that – literally. Predictably, David let her

down, but Cindy found herself a new bloke in Italy who worshipped the ground she walked on – until she was arrested for attempted murder. Faced with proof of what Cindy was capable of, he left her to rot in jail, even though she was carrying his child. Tragically, she died of a pulmonary embolism while giving birth. RIP, Cindy.

SEE ALSO:
Donna Ludlow, James Willmott-Brown

Pat & Roy Evans

Born 14.06.35
(Tony Caunter)

Born 28.12.42
(Pam St. Clement)

She was Mrs Pete Beale, then Mrs Brian Wicks, then Mrs Frank Butcher and is now Mrs Roy Evans

Pat was once a buxom beauty, a Diana Dors lookalike who, as a teenager, won a Miss Butlins competition and captivated the young Frank Butcher's heart. Her love affair with Frank has continued, on and off, ever since, and although they're both happy with their respective partners there's still a flicker between them when she orders a G&T. Fifty-eight-year-old Pat was born a Harris and has acquired four different surnames since. She was Mrs Pete Beale, then Mrs Brian Wicks, then Mrs Frank Butcher and is now Mrs Roy Evans. In-between (and, frequently, during) these marriages she has played the field with a sweeper system all of her own, though she has been loyal to Roy – since she married him, anyway. She's a straight-talker and very practical, although even Pat found it hard to pull herself together after Frank disappeared leaving her a mountain of debts. Pat's no stranger to adversity; she spent four months in prison after running down and killing a teenage girl in her cab after a couple of drinks on Christmas Eve 1992. Because of her past, Pat is less likely to judge than many people in the Square and can be relied on to keep a secret (Irene's toyboy, Bianca's affair). She has notoriously bad taste in soft furnishings but a good head for figures, wears outlandish earrings and can't – according to Peggy – make sausage rolls, but when it comes to a crisis, Pat's a safe bet. Unless it's catering for an emergency buffet!

'Honest' Roy Evans has always been a bit of a bumbler, but he's never been known to do anything dodgy – that is, until Phil Mitchell coaxed him over to the Dark Side. Now Roy, beset by financial worries and Pat's hankering for holidays and health farms, has agreed to sell his soul to the devil and go in with Phil on a lucrative car-ringing scam. The likelihood of this bringing the poor sucker health, wealth and happiness is low. Well-meaning Roy has never been very lucky with money: he had to sell his thriving car dealership at Manor Wood for a pittance after son Barry was fleeced by fake fiancée Vanessa. Working to make up for that brought on a heart attack, and with the car lot going down the tubes he decided to end it all by throwing himself off the top of a multi-storey car park. Love-rival Frank Butcher saved his bacon by talking him out of it and investing in Roy's business, which is why Roy is feeling a tad guilty about going behind his back. But then Roy's always been big on guilt. He was having sex with another woman when his wife Doreen died in childbirth, along with his baby daughter, rendering him impotent for the next 28 years. He leapt at the chance offered by (black market) Viagra, which made him breathless and panicky before he got anywhere near second wife Pat, and was referred for counselling. This eventually did the trick but Barry wouldn't speak to Roy for almost a month after learning about his infidelity. Heaven help Pat if Roy gets caught in the act with stolen cars: the guilt might put paid to marital relations permanently.

Well-meaning Roy has never been very lucky with money

Since the Millennium double wedding, Barry has been floating several feet above the ground like a large, Hawaiian-print helium balloon. He's bound to come down to earth with a bump again soon because Barry, being Barry, has a talent for stuffing things up rivalled only by Ricky Butcher and, arguably, Robbie Jackson. Like the wedding, in fact, which very nearly didn't happen at all after Barry and Nat's frightful mum got carried away with their tacky, Creation-themed extravaganza, causing the bride-to-be to freak. Barry's a buffoon, but underneath his floral shirts beats a heart of gold. (OK, he used foul means to win the job of video-shop manager over Robbie, but then Robbie got his own back with his Best Man's speech.) Barry was one of the few people to speak up for Cindy Beale at her funeral, because, as he said, she treated him as a person, not a joke. The fact that he gave her a safe house when she left Ian and helped her kidnap the kids probably had something to do with that. Barry is easily exploited and tends to act first and think later, hence his capacity for getting into trouble. It was Barry who torched the car lot the second time around, nearly killing Phil, because he wanted to help his struggling father out. He also fell prey to grifter Vanessa, who got engaged to him and then stung the Evans's for a fortune before fleeing the country. Will he wise up now he's got the lovely Natalie? Let's hope not; Barry's too much fun for that.

Barry & Natalie Evans

Born 01.09.61
(Shaun Williamson)

Born 12.03.77
(Lucy Speed)

This may be one EastEnders marriage that ends happily ever after

Andrea Price

Born 1952
(Cindy O'Callaghan)

Having stayed in the shadows most of her life, Natalie Price seemed an unlikely candidate for Bride of the Year, but then it's time she had a little glory. There's no comparison between the radiant woman who married Barry Evans at the Millennium double wedding and the weeping girl who was drummed out of the Square by a screaming Bianca back in 1995 (*above left*). Bianca, who discovered Ricky and Natalie – her second-best friend (Tiffany was always number one) – making out in the Arches, spared her no quarter; the entire Jackson family was roped into a vendetta against Natalie and it was four years before she dared show her face again. When she did, it was as a sassy, besuited, professional woman who had got her act together and started up her own business, a dating agency. Bianca, spitting nails, warned her off her patch and her man, but this time Nat refused to be intimidated and they eventually bonded after Ricky had an accident. The old closeness was never quite the same, though; Bianca didn't confide in her about her affair with Dan, and when the scandal broke, Natalie refused to support her. The tables turned, a friendless B slunk out of town while Natalie discovered true love with Barry. Since this has survived sabotage by her mother, the appalling Andrea, on two occasions now, not to mention Barry's habit of making a fist of things, we should take heart: this may be one *EastEnders* marriage that ends happily ever after. Well, one can dream.

Natalie's interfering mother-from-hell, a blowsy, boozy divorcee long past her sell-by date, harbours pathetic illusions about her own youthful attractiveness. She alternated between neglecting and bullying her youngest daughter when Natalie was growing up, and constantly makes it clear she isn't good enough – at anything. Elder daughter Susie, a hairdresser, has always been the preferred one, and the two of them like nothing better than to pick holes in poor Nat. Barry, ignoring Natalie's protests, insisted on dragging her home to meet Andrea for himself and nearly lost his girlfriend after a weekend of cocktails, carping and catfights – a kind of *Abigail's Party* meets Tennessee Williams. Never one to learn from his mistakes, Barry persuaded Natalie to let her mum help out with the wedding and almost blew it again when Andrea took over. After humiliating Natalie on her hen night, Mrs Price and her entourage were restrained from stealing the show at the wedding (Susie tried and failed to foist her son into the proceedings as a pageboy) and Andrea has since been put back in her chintzy suburban box. However, it seems unlikely to be her last appearance; she's too horribly hilarious for that.

David Wicks

Born 21.04.62
(Michael French)

David Wicks had the kind of animal magnetism most men dream of. A careerist Casanova, he began early at 14, when he got young Carol Branning, also 14, pregnant. He paid for her to have an abortion but unbeknown to him she didn't go through with it. A consequence of this was that when David turned up in the Square for his father Pete's funeral, he found himself fancying his own 17-year-old daughter, Bianca Jackson, an attraction he was deeply disturbed by and fought hard to quell. To take his mind off it, he began an affair with Cindy Beale, but ended it when she became obsessive and demanding. On a lads' trip to Spain, by freakish coincidence, David met and bedded Sam Mitchell, but she proved too bloodless for his taste and he returned to nymphomaniac Cindy. This time, though, David had bitten off more than even he could chew. Cindy started talking about killing husband Ian, and David, back-pedalling on his promises, found himself taking refuge in the arms of Carol, now married and a mother of four. It was only with Carol that David became vaguely human, but even she couldn't save him from himself. He was feckless, weak, dishonest and couldn't commit to relationships for a month, let alone marriage (to Lorraine) and kids (Karen and Joe), which had proved a total disaster. When Joe ran away from home to be with him after his sister's death, David failed him utterly, deserting the schizophrenic teenager at the height of his illness and driving off never to return. For all his snappy suits and sleek hair, he was just a sheep in wolf's clothing.

Simon Wicks

Born 07.07.65
(Nick Berry)

Like his elder brother David, 'Wicksy' (as he was known to everyone), was a smoothie and a charmer and just as shallow, lazy and unreliable. Both graduated from the 'love 'em and leave 'em' school of relationships and Wicksy began breaking hearts almost as soon as he swung into the Square in his showy yellow sports car. Having dallied with Naima, Magda, Cindy and Donna, he started going out with Sharon Watts, who fell deeply in love with him. They ran the Vic together and Sharon was keen to go for the tenancy, but it was all too much like hard work for shiftless Simon, who couldn't cope with commitment to either Sharon or the pub. Meanwhile, Cindy had married Ian Beale and given birth to Simon's baby (Steven), who Wicksy had originally refused to acknowledge as his. Maybe it was because he had only found out who his own father was two years ago – Brian Wicks, not Kenny or Pete, who he thought of as his dad – but something made Wicksy change his mind and he belatedly decided to make a go of things with Cindy (*above*). Ian went bonkers and tried to discredit him any way he could, even making a botched attempt on his life, and the couple finally fled Walford with baby Steven (*above*). Since then, we've only heard snippets about Wicksy. Predictably, he grew tired of being a dad and dumped his little family. He has made no effort to contact Steven and recently emigrated to Canada.

Lorraine & Joe Wicks

Born 07.07.60

(Jacqueline Leonard)

Born 26.08.80

(Paul Nicholls)

Lorraine had a head of shaggy curls, cheekbones as sharp as scythes and no bottom to speak of. Naturally, she looked stunning. She was also so relentlessly sensible, fair and nice that one could only put her choice of men down to a rogue gene. Why else would such a lovely girl marry David Wicks? Sure he was sexy, but he had 'chancer' written all over him, and Lorraine was a bright girl, smart enough to spot that. She did, eventually, after he'd had numerous affairs, and divorced him, but not until they'd had two children (Karen and Joe). Even more perplexing was why she fell for Grant Mitchell. Perhaps she thought she could change him. Perhaps Grant thought she could change him. He did really make an effort to be restrained, but maintaining this facade was beyond him and, after seeing Grant shake her son so hard that his teeth rattled, Lorraine called the whole thing off. Originally, she had come south to Walford to track down the errant Joe, taking a job in the Vic to pay her way. Joe's emotional instability was hard for Lorraine to cope with: she'd lost his sister in a car crash and Karen's death had affected mother and son very deeply. Joe's behaviour turned increasingly bizarre and destructive and, after holding Lorraine hostage in their flat, he was diagnosed as schizophrenic and sectioned. When he finally got better, Lorraine returned to Bolton and was reunited with her guitarist boyfriend Peter who was sweet, supportive and didn't shake people, thus coming to her senses at last.

Nobody knew Joe was schizophrenic when he turned up in the Square looking for his father, David, and to start with, the handsome youngster didn't appear disturbed. True, he was moody and angry, but he started school in Walford, made friends with Sarah Hills and everything seemed to be OK. Then David found a dead cat under his bed. From then on, Joe's decline became marked. He became obsessed with aliens, wrapped the TV in tinfoil, plastered newspaper cuttings all over his bedroom, developed paranoia about poisoning and pronounced Grant Mitchell Evil Incarnate in a bleakly humorous Christmas turkey-carving scene. He was given drugs for depression but stopped taking them and became steadily worse, once trying to commit suicide and finally barricading Lorraine in her flat. After being sectioned Joe was correctly diagnosed as schizophrenic and given the right treatment. (At the root of his mental illness was his crushing guilt about the death of his sister Karen, whom he'd swapped seats with before the crash that killed her.) Joe and Sarah remained close, their friendship blossoming into love after he was discharged from the hospital, and they eventually got engaged, although he did have a reluctant one-night stand with Irish girl Mary. It wasn't just Sarah and Mary who went teary-eyed when the gorgeous Joe left to go home to Bolton: teenage girls up and down the land went into mourning, too.

SEE ALSO:
Carol Jackson, Bianca Butcher, Pete Beale, Cindy Beale

Sensible Sonia has always been the voice of reason in the vociferous Jackson mob. She's an intelligent, astute, deeply sensitive girl with a strong sense of family, despite – or more probably, because of – her and her siblings' different fathers. She never knew her own father and has always regarded Alan Jackson as her dad, so when he and Carol broke up she felt her world was falling apart. Sonia adores babies and pestered Bianca

An intelligent, astute, deeply sensitive girl with a strong sense of family

Jackson

Sonia

Born 06.05.85

(Natalie Cassidy)

to let her be little Liam's godmother, wearing her down until she agreed and even organising the christening. She was thrilled when she found out her mother Carol was expecting and totally devastated when Bianca's affair with Dan resulted not only in her sister and Liam moving away but Carol terminating the pregnancy. Sonia's had to grow up fast because of this and is learning to develop a hard shell to protect her tender feelings, especially now that most of her family aren't around her any more. A plain, plump schoolgirl, Sonia's always known she can't compete with her pretty mates Nicky (*above, right*) and Kim in the looks department (though she's much brighter than them) and was bowled over when Italian exchange student Enrico preferred her company. Not only had she found a boy who shared her passion for playing the trumpet, but he was gorgeous, romantic and a great kisser. They swore to love each other, but Valentine's Day came and went with no word from Enrico, which does not bode well. Welcome to the world of relationships, Sonia, sweetheart.

Robbie Jackson

Robbie could never be described as a catch

Born 18.10.78

(Dean Gaffney)

It's hard to believe Robbie Jackson's now 21. He's come on considerably from the spotty, surly, lank-haired youth who first turned up in the Square with the rest of the Jackson family in 1993. Carol's eldest son was a teenage tearaway, frequently playing truant, occasionally shoplifting and generally making a nuisance of himself. This aspect of Robbie's character was toned down and the unfortunate Robbie became less of a lout and more of – there is no way of saying this kindly – a prat, forever mucking things up and being the fall guy. (Best man Robbie couldn't even stitch up groom Barry, *below*, on his stag night properly. It was Robbie who ended up paralytic with a henna

tattoo...) While his relationships with humans tend towards the disastrous, Robbie has always got on well with animals and adopted a mangy German Shepherd dog, Wellard (geddit?). Robbie could never be described as a catch (except in the contagious disease sense) and he's never had a proper girlfriend. He did it once with Sarah Hills, who immediately regretted her temporary insanity and ran off in tears, resulting in her father jumping to the wrong conclusion and hospitalising him. After that Robbie's sexual encounters were non-existent until a whirlwind weekend in Brighton in 1999, when he unexpectedly got off with Becky, a kooky, kinky student who played more than pinball with him in a video arcade. Despite his erratic education, Robbie has turned out to be a good worker and runs the café surprisingly well. When Carol and Alan split up he became the responsible male in the family and is very protective of his sister Sonia, with whom he lives (along with Ricky and Grandpa Jim) in the now depleted Jackson house.

JimBranning

Born 1933

(John Bardon)

A watered-down version of Alf Garnett, Robbie and Sonia's grandpa is a wrinkly letch and a racist old bigot of the 'I blame foreigners' variety. He first appeared in 1996, refusing to give Carol away and storming out after Alan sprang his proposal on her at April's wedding. Jim resurfaced in June 1999, when Carol, who had been estranged from him ever since, visited him at a care home in Brighton with new bloke Dan. After his wife Rene died, Jim moved in to the Jackson house, by which time Carol had already left to pick up the threads of family life with Billy and Alan. Jim's been a semi-invalid for much of his working life following a fall (drunk) from a bedroom window, but he can get about and, until a few years ago, had a job collecting supermarket trolleys. Since he arrived in the Square it's not taken him long to get into a routine: he has apparently taken root in the café, where he spends his time annoying Robbie and keeping up a running commentary on everything going on. Evenings are spent down the pub – Jim's been a boozer since his labouring days – and he has already become absorbed into Frank's little after-hours gaming circle. He has a big mouth, slavers disgracefully after women, pinches bums, is offensive and a social liability – not at all PC, but someone needs to give tamed Terry Raymond a run for his money...

Significant others

April

Born 1961

(Debbie Arnold)

April, Carol's sister, was like her name – blonde, soft and sunny, with big blue eyes and a sweet voice. Like a breath of spring air, she breezed into the Square in December 1995 to invite Carol and Alan to her wedding. Carol, who hadn't seen her sister for eight years – April had been living in Greece, where she met and got engaged to the infamous Nikos – initially refused, knowing the reception Alan would get from her racist father, but eventually decided to go and stand up to the old man. When April was jilted at the altar by Nikos, she insisted that Alan go through with his plan to pop the question to Carol, telling him it was the only thing that would cheer her up. That was the last we saw of April for three months, when she turned up again and was instantly attracted to market inspector Michael Rose (what

She had obviously never heard the warning about Greeks bearing gifts

Branning

Blossom was Alan's gran, a robust Tobagan woman who originally came to Britain on a ship with her parents – actually she was born on the ship – and grew up in the East End of London. When Blossom's common-law husband, Bill, died in 1993 (her real husband, Nathan, had deserted her years earlier), she was left alone in their tiny Wapping terrace, becoming increasingly agoraphobic as the rest of the street was torn down by developers. Alan became concerned after Blossom was burgled and eventually persuaded her to move in with him and Carol. With four kids, 25 Albert Square was already cramped and Bianca in particular resented having to make room. Blossom, however, took none of B's lip and also proved more than a match for Tiffany (who swelled numbers further by kipping on the couch), making her earn her keep at the café. Even at 68, Blossom, who'd been a wild girl in her youth, could still mix it with the Square's more senior singles. She

is it with that man?). Deciding to stay, April got herself a job in the café, where she was witness to Frankie's ensnaring of Alan and reluctantly told her sister. After three months, lovestruck Michael begged her to move in with him, throwing April into a quandary. Fortunately, Nikos the rat turned up the next day protesting his love and demanding to marry her after all. April, who had obviously never heard the warning about Greeks bearing gifts, went off with him and this time got him up the aisle successfully, leaving Michael to marshal his stalls and mull over what might have been.

Blossom Jackson

Born 29.07.26

(Mona Hammond)

dated Jules Tavernier *(above)*, moving in with him temporarily after the Jackson's house was damaged in a gas explosion, and they ended up sharing a bed (although all they did was play Scrabble!). Blossom later became friends with Jewish barber Felix Kawalski, and when he asked her to accompany him to Israel, she seized the opportunity for the adventure of a lifetime and went with him. The hint of romance between them remained just that, and Blossom has since returned and is living with Alan and Billy.

Youngest of the Jackson Four, Billy was a cheeky, curly-haired cherub whose principal dramatic function seemed to be to generate angst in the bosom of his family. On Christmas Day 1996 he ran off, upset that his father Alan wasn't at home (this was during the Frankie period), prompting most of the Square to abandon their turkey to look for him. He was eventually found by Nigel sitting in a derelict building, but nobody begrudged him their congealed sprouts because Billy was so angelic. His next disappearance lasted longer and was much more frightening – he was snatched from the school playground and held hostage because he was able to identify

Carol Jackson

Born 03.10.62

(Lindsey Coulson)

Billy Jackson

Born 15.10.88

(Devon Anderson)

one of the robbers in a raid on a building society that he'd witnessed. Carol Jackson made a courageous televised appeal and Billy was tracked down several days later, unharmed. With the Jacksons still receiving threats, Carol, Alan, Blossom, Sonia and Billy agreed to be relocated for their own safety, but since then Billy has seen less and less of his siblings. After Carol and Alan broke up, Alan applied for custody of Billy and Carol reluctantly decided not to contest it. Billy now receives regular visits from his mother and she even spent Christmas with him.

Carol always looked careworn and sounded snappish, but then, as she pointed out repeatedly, she's had to make a lot of sacrifices in her life, raising four kids single-handedly, missing out on any chance of a career, etc, etc. She began early, aged just 14, when David Wicks got her up the duff, resulting in Bianca. This sparked a major feud between the Wicks's and the Brannings, hence the prickliness between Pat and Carol. When the Jacksons moved to Albert Square, Carol was with common-law husband Alan, by whom she had Billy (Robbie and Sonia came in-between; they each have different fathers who Carol never much talked about). Things declined after Alan married her; Carol's constant bitching drove him into the arms of manipulative minx Frankie (*above, right*) and Carol, in turn, got together with old flame David. Then, in 1997, Billy witnessed a robbery and was kidnapped. He was found safe, but the family was forced to go into witness protection until after the trial and we didn't see Carol again until 1999, when she reappeared, glowing, with a new fella – Dan. Unfortunately, he was also Bianca's ex. Bianca and Dan rekindled their passion which, with the inevitability of a Greek tragedy, ruined everyone's lives. Fuelled by a blistering sense of betrayal, Carol

Jackson Alan

Born 22.11.67

(Howard Antony)

Alan stayed around uniting the family and giving Carol stability

A lan Jackson was 20, single and a plumber when he met Carol. He came to her council flat to unblock her sink – Carol was between plungers at the time – and never left. Pretty soon he had added to her collection of three kids, fathering Billy, but unlike the disparate dads who had come before, Alan stayed around, uniting the family and giving Carol a stability she hadn't experienced up 'til then. Even though he and Carol weren't married, they all took Alan's surname; he made this official at her sister April's wedding, proposing to Carol in the church and marrying her on the spot (the vicar had been primed!). Despite this wildly romantic gesture, it didn't stop the rot setting in. Carol was a difficult woman to live with and they had frequent rows, especially about money – Alan was unemployed and his attempts to get work were rarely successful. His confidence undermined, and stung by Carol's carping, vulnerable Alan walked straight into the honey trap laid by scheming singer Frankie. Carol found out and gave him the boot and, having got what she wanted, Frankie did too. Alan was miserable without Carol, but she refused to have him back and it took Robbie being attacked by Ted to reunite the couple. Since the Jacksons left Walford we haven't seen Alan again, but we do know that he had some sort of nervous breakdown and that he and Carol subsequently split up again. However, since Carol's calamitous experience with Dan she has grown to appreciate steady Alan's good qualities and now has a civil, friendly, non-sexual relationship with him.

rejected her daughter, dumped Dan, aborted his child and then fell apart at the seams. The scenes were gruelling and savage and genuinely moving, marking the end of the line for mother and daughter. Bianca slunk off to Manchester and Carol, reeling from yet another blow – her mother's imminent death – packed up and left. She's since had a reconciliation of sorts with Alan and is living in Balham near him and Billy.

SEE ALSO:
Bianca Butcher (aka Jackson), David Wicks, Dan Sullivan, Frankie Pierre

Terry & Irene Raymond

Born 18.04.49
(Gavin Richards)

Born 30.06.48
(Roberta Taylor)

Terry's reputation preceded him long before he turned up in the Square. He was the monster who had beaten his gay son Simon and pushed his pregnant daughter Tiffany down the stairs, causing her to miscarry. Tiffany was terrified of him and not at all sympathetic when she heard that her father was in hospital with pancreatitis (caused by years of heavy drinking), although after he was readmitted she relented and visited him, fearing he would die (particularly noble considering a ranting Terry had tried to disrupt Tiff and Grant's Blessing). Before they knew it, Tiff and Simon had been put in charge of their father's recuperation and Terry had smooth-talked his way into staying at the Vic. It wasn't long before Grant 'persuaded' Terry to move on, but by then anyway he had met Irene Hills, who fell for his charm (Terry had once been a successful estate agent; buttering up was his forte) and offered him her sofa. Suffice to say, he did not stay downstairs for long. Since then, Terry has undergone something of a sea-change, becoming a clumsy, comical, almost (whisper it) sympathetic character. He's given up the booze and the nags – another of his weaknesses (although it was having a flutter that scooped him the money to buy the First 'til Last) – and is trying his best to please Iron Irene. He truly loves her, but he's hopeless at showing it and his romantic gestures (such as they are) have a tendency to backfire on him. Still, he kept shtoom about her affair with Troy, which, given Terry's propensity for putting his foot in his mouth, can't have been easy. Terry Raymond – Mr Sensitive? Surely not!

He's given up the booze and the nags – another of his weaknesses... and is trying his best to please Iron Irene

It was Troy's own brand of complementary therapy that ultimately unblocked her meridians

settlement. After being fleeced by a conman, Irene came to the Square and moved in with Sarah and Tony, deciding, belatedly, to do her 'good mother' bit. Before long she'd set her sights on Terry, who spun her a line about his non-existent wealth, but when she discovered the truth Irene agreed to marry him anyway. The wedding was the most humiliating day of her life: Terry's wife, Louise, who he'd never divorced, marched in and denounced him to the entire congregation. Terry and Irene went on their honeymoon to escape the gossip and he later married her secretly at a registry office. They've always had an up-and-down relationship and, on a hilarious jaunt into the country, both were tempted to stray, but it was Irene who ended up rocking the boat with youthful lodger Troy (*below*). After Terry warned him off, the couple went on a second honeymoon to patch things up. Let's hope they're not too successful, or they won't be half as much fun.

The Square's unlikeliest sex siren, 51-year-old Irene has been making waves – and a lot else beside – with a toyboy less than half her age, giving renewed hope to all women on the verge of HRT. Irene, of course, didn't actually have HRT; when the menopause hit she tried herbal tea, Tai Chi and Feng Shui, but it was Troy's own brand of complementary therapy that ultimately unblocked her meridians. Perhaps we shouldn't be surprised: Irene's always been restless – she and her first husband, Ted Hills, were equally unfaithful and when their marriage fell apart she abandoned her children, Tony and Sarah, and lived it up on the proceeds of her divorce

Simon Raymond

Born 10.12.74

(Andrew Lynford)

He was open about his sexuality and once stood up in the Vic announcing he was gay and proud of it

When last heard of, Simon was backpacking round Europe with Tony Hills (*right*), his on-off-on-again bisexual boyfriend. The pair have already travelled a rocky road: they first got together when Tony was with Tiffany, and although she was shocked at the betrayal – she caught them kissing – they all ended up sharing a tiny flat, the ultimate odd threesome. Brother and sister had always been close, having bonded under father Terry's tyranny, so Tiffany was relaxed about Simon's set-up. He had come out to her when he was 18, and she often gave him relationship advice, in particular telling him to leave his previous boyfriend, Howard, who was violent. (In fact, that was what made Simon come to live in Walford.) Simon had a background in clothes retailing and got a job on Sanjay and Gita's stall, and, when they went, Bianca's. He was open about his sexuality and once stood up in the Vic, announcing he was gay and proud of it, upsetting the less assured Tony. They broke up after Tony began an affair with a journalist, Polly, but Simon never really got over him even though he dated other men. When Tiffany died he withdrew into himself, obsessing about getting revenge on Grant and, on one occasion, abducting his god-daughter Courtney (*left*). After getting drunk and accidentally setting fire to Louise's flat, Simon suffered severe burns and was sent to a special unit, where he made a full recovery. He and Tony left soon afterwards following a great deal of will-they-won't-they dithering that fooled no-one but themselves.

Louise was not really a nice person. She simpered and postured and anguished about things, then went ahead and did them anyway, causing untold pain to her children, Simon and Tiffany. Granted, marriage to Terry Raymond was no picnic: while he was successful, things were OK, but when the eighties bubble burst and the housing market collapsed, taking the Raymonds' lifestyle with it, Terry changed and became a violent drunk. Louise got out, leaving her children behind, and Tiff and Simon took the brunt of their father's anger instead. They never forgave her for it. When Louise turned up in Walford, it was not so much to heal that rift as to grab what she could of Terry's lucrative win on the horses. Still, she managed to win Simon and Tiffany round, and when she next appeared – having dumped her toyboy, Gary – Tiffany was an emotional wreck and appreciated having her

She was half-heartedly dating Gianni di Marco while eyeing Grant up for herself

Louise Raymond

Born 13.09.58

(Carol Harrison)

mother's shoulder to cry on. After one outburst too many from Grant, Tiff moved out of the Vic and in with Louise, who was half-heartedly dating Gianni di Marco while eyeing Grant up for herself. The inevitable happened one rainy afternoon when Louise and Grant (*above*) made love after Tiff's birthday party, but Tiff didn't find out until she and Grant had been reunited. The betrayal shattered her world and she died trying to escape from it. When Simon found out about his mother and Grant he became clinically depressed and was almost killed in a fire. Grant wouldn't have anything more to do with Louise and she was eventually hounded out of the Square by Bianca, who thought it the least she could do in memory of her best mate. No-one waved goodbye.

Rosa di Marco

Born 02.07.51

(Louise Jameson)

EastEnders already had two matriarchs fighting to outdo each other when the di Marcos moved into the Square, but since comely Italian widow Rosa threw her cap into the ring, Peggy and Pauline have had their work cut out to compete. No sooner had Rosa opened up her restaurant, Giuseppes, than she was telling Pauline how to make a marinade and criticising Peggy's steak-and-kidney. There was a thawing of relations on Christmas Day 1998 when Rosa cooked everyone's turkeys,

but by last Christmas, with the Mitchells coming to dinner, it was open season again. It has never helped matters that Peggy's former fiancé, George Palmer, had a 'thing' for Rosa. Shady George, the di Marcos' business partner, had once slept with Rosa when her husband, Giuseppe, was in prison (for tax evasion). He thought her second son, Gianni, was his (he wasn't). George proposed in November 1998, hoping to make the relationship with Gianni official, and although Rosa agreed to marry him, she saw through his motives and changed her mind. She also turned down Jeff Healy, something she now rather regrets – especially as Pauline's snaffled him – and was amused but unmoved by toyboy Troy's advances.

Rosa's found life increasingly lonely and is throwing her energies into playing the traditional Italian mama

Since then, Rosa's found life increasingly lonely and is throwing her energies into playing the traditional Italian mama. She was surprisingly enthusiastic about expanding the family business into the Vic and viewed both Sam and Jackie as suitable potential daughters-in-law. However, when Sandra, Beppe's ex – who had never knuckled down to the wifely role expected of her – turned up, hot-blooded Rosa flew at her with her claws out. Which goes to show, if you don't know your fusilli from your foccacia, she'll have you for breakfast, probably on a nice slice of lightly toasted ciabatta.

Gianni di Marco

Born 04.04.71

(Marc Bannerman)

Gianni may act like a hunk with half a brain, but his idea to save Giuseppes by introducing takeaways worked, so there must be a light shining somewhere inside that thick skull. In fact, shallow Gianni has been showing signs of having hidden depths since he took up with Jackie Owen. Until then he was just a pretty playboy with a line in corny come-ons; now he's devoted, sensitive, caring and thoughtful. Unless he's been switched by aliens, it's got to be love. This is surprising, because most of Gianni's relationships haven't lasted longer than one night. He did allow himself to fall for Annie Palmer, but after they slept together it blew up in his face when George – who Gianni had always loathed – revealed he might be his father. Blood tests proved he wasn't, but by then Annie couldn't hack things and called it off. Louise Raymond dated him half-heartedly with one eye on Grant, but after Tiffany's death she became clingy and demanding, provoking Gianni (who was sticking up for Beppe) to be viciously cruel about her age. Gianni returned to playing the field, seducing and then losing interest in Lisa, but his smooth chat did nothing for Jackie, who knocked him back publicly when they first met. She came to work at Giuseppe's and they remained at loggerheads until the Arches collapsed on top of them, giving them the chance for a real heart-to-heart. Gianni tried to kiss her, nearly killing the pair of them with falling masonry, and since then they've been inseparable. Amazing what a bump on the head can do.

B eppe is Rosa's gorgeous eldest son and has always been terribly spoiled by her. No wonder: one look into those melting chocolate eyes and most women would do anything for him – except, apparently, tarty Tiffany *(below left)*, who put on his handcuffs, took off her clothes and then decided it was gorilla Grant she loved after all. No wonder Beppe hated the Mitchells. For Beppe, it was the real thing with Tiff and when she died he burned her letter exonerating Grant, determined to make him pay. This got the Vice Squad copper kicked out of the Met and, after a succession of stultifying jobs, he bought into E20, not least to rub Grant's nose in it. Since then Beppe, who has always been straight, has become marginally more flexible in his outlook (requesting a police colleague to turn a blind eye to some drugs that were planted in the

Beppe di Marco

Born 23.07.70
(Michael Greco)

club) and is even coming round to working with Steve Owen. Disillusioned after Tiff, he still managed to repeat the mistake by falling for another Mitchell – Sam – hiking Grant's blood pressure even further and prompting the bruvs to declare all-out war. But the spark with Sam was only ever fleeting – Beppe has always got on better with his lodger, Nina – and what had looked like love at first sight cooled when Sam closed ranks. It then fizzled out completely after Beppe's estranged wife, Sandra, reappeared. Sandra is on a par with the anti-Christ in di Marco circles, especially now she's filing for custody of their son, 8-year-old Joe *(right)*, but Beppe still fancies her and the torment is making him look more like an injured puppy than ever. Ahhh.

Sandra di Marco

Born 27.08.73

(Clare Wilkie)

Sandra's a di Marco by marriage only, and even when she was with Beppe she was never really accepted by the rest of the family, who couldn't forgive her for not being Italian. This was what drove her to leave Beppe and her son, Little Joe (*left*). Sandra had always wanted a career and she went back to work after having Joe, incurring further disapproval, particularly from the grandparents, Nonno and Nonna, and Rosa. Eventually their hostility became too much and when Beppe took sides with his family, Sandra felt isolated and miserable. Deciding she wasn't cut out to play the little Italian wife, she upped and left, abandoning Joe, who was only a year old at the time. As far as the family was concerned it was good riddance, although Beppe was deeply hurt. No-one's heard anything from her until recently, when she reappeared on the di Marco's doorstep, sending the whole family into panic mode. But is Sandra really the witch she's made out to be? Rosa's pathological hatred of her is simply jealousy – Sandra stole her little boy from her – and as for Beppe, methinks he doth protest too much. He clearly still fancies the pants off her. Admittedly, Sandra's attempts to see her son haven't been handled well – the sneaky encounter in the museum and the kidnap-attempt-that-wasn't have done nothing to bolster trust – but is there any need for lawyers and custody battles and the whole song-and-dance? Of course there is. They're Italian. This is a soap. Enough said.

Teresa di Marco

Born 14.10.80

(Leila Birch)

She's managed to break out of the restaurant by dint of persistence and subterfuge

Teresa's a hothead who gets off on danger and rebelling against her smothering family. She's an expert liar and specialises in two expressions – wounded innocence and teeth-gnashing outrage – with very little in-between. Like Beppe, she's managed to break out of the restaurant by dint of persistence and subterfuge, and now runs Bianca's stall. She'll try anything for a laugh and frequently gets herself into trouble, which her brothers then have to bail her out of. Neither of them approved of her seeing bisexual Tony Hills, and when the pair were busted in a drugs raid on a Norfolk pub, Beppe used his influence to get Teresa off on condition that she stopped seeing Tony. (In fact, the charges had been dropped.) She moved on to Lenny, incurring Gianni's wrath, not – as Teresa thought – because he was racist, but because he recognised Lenny as a womaniser and didn't want his little sis getting hurt. Undeterred, Teresa tempted Ricky Butcher to go Christmas-tree rustling with her and then snogged him in a darkened doorway, frightening the poor lad out of his few remaining wits. They shared a bed together on New Year's Eve, although Ricky had passed out with booze and nothing happened. Teresa's biggest mistake was to fall for Matthew Rose *(above)*, who started off as a cool DJ and ended up as a madman, having been driven to extreme measures by being banged up for killing Saskia. She went on the run with him, stood by him in prison and helped plot the wind-up on Steve, but when Matthew started waving petrol cans, it was too much danger, even for an adrenaline junkie like her.

'Nicky', as she's always known, was a surprise fourth child and has always been the apple of her mother's eye. A schoolgirl, she's pretty and popular but spoiled and manipulative – although not in the same league as Janine Butcher, who is clearly going to lead her into bad ways. Sonia used to be Nicky's best friend, but since Nicky tried to swipe Enrico from under her nose, Sonia has become more wary of her. Nicky's a hit with boys

Nicoletta di Marco

Born 25.12.85
(Carly Hillman)

and dated Jamie Mitchell for a while, before moving on to Asif Malik and then Martin Fowler. She's been smart enough to stay out of trouble so far, giving Asif hell for exaggerating what they did and dropping Martin when he tried it on after telling her he loved her. She's not particularly bright academically and is having trouble with her maths – small wonder when elder sister Teresa puts two and two together and constantly makes five. Teresa, seeing Nicky upset over Martin's deception, has been trying to give her the benefit of her own sexual experience, although whether this is going to be helpful remains to be seen.

Significant others

Luisa and Bruno – or Nonna and Nonno (Italian for grandmother and grandfather) as they were always called by their family – had taken over the family restaurant in Soho started by Bruno's father and eventually gave it to Giuseppe, Rosa's husband, as a wedding present. Bruno, who had terrible bronchitis due to his smoking and couldn't work, liked to hold court at his favourite table, playing cards and passing comments, while Luisa

looked after Rosa and Giuseppe's children and later brought up Little Joe after Sandra's moonlight flit. Both were raised in London and had little direct knowledge of their homeland, and they didn't even speak Italian that well, but for them, as with all the di Marcos, being Italian was everything. The

Luisa & Bruno di Marco

Born 15.03.29
(Stella Tanner)

Born 01.08.27
(Leon Lissek)

elderly couple had only been in Walford a year before Luisa suffered a stroke (this was when Teresa was in Norfolk with Tony, and Beppe and Gianni came looking for her thinking Luisa was going to die). She recovered sufficiently to come out of hospital but remained frail, and in December 1998 Bruno told an unhappy Rosa that they were taking a trip to the old country before it was too late. They rang a few weeks later, having decided to stay in Italy, but Luisa's cooking still managed to have repercussions in Walford: a salami that she sent back was responsible for the bout of food poisoning that closed the Night Café and lost Mick his job.

George Palmer was a gentleman, the smoothest of smooth operators. You never saw him roll up his sleeves, or even take off his bespoke jacket. All George did was click his fingers and whoever had earned his ire was seen to. Quite how was never spelt out, but George Palmer's name carried serious clout in the criminal underworld, or it did when he started seeing Peggy Mitchell. Not that she knew any of

George Palmer

Born 08.02.46

(Paul Moriarty)

this. George's original motive for schmoozing Peggy was pragmatic – he was trying to stop her petition against the Cobra Club (an arm of his money laundering operation) – but he was genuinely attracted to her. The closer they became, the more he tried to protect her from the illegal side of his work, although Grant and Phil, who were more sussed, both got in on the action. She was on the point of marrying him when Phil, realising he and Annie had put her in danger (by using George's name in their underworld dealings) told Peggy the truth. Peggy gave George the boot and he went to New Zealand, where his 'import/export' business was based, to lick his wounds. When

George returned, a furious Peggy – who had been menaced by masked men looking for him in his absence – would have nothing to do with him and he renewed his attentions to old flame Rosa, who he'd bailed out of her failing restaurant in Soho and set up in Walford. However, everything fell apart after the Gianni business and, having lost a second fiancée, George called it quits and went back to New Zealand for good.

Hard-nosed Annie Palmer was a rather terrifying creation, a kind of dominatrix without the dungeon. A verbal Miss Whiplash, she tore strips off anyone who crossed her and ran the Market Cellar, George's club/illegal gambling den, with a rod of iron. She was smart, perceptive and stunning to look at, and not averse to using her femininity as a weapon. Annie got results – in bed and in business – but her toughness masked a desperate vulnerability, and for that reason she rarely allowed men to get close. She made a pass at Grant and then played Phil and Conor off against each other, basically to show them who was boss. Gianni (below), who had known Annie since childhood, made some headway, but the thought that their relationship could have been incestuous freaked her out. It was fellow traveller Steve Owen who got through her prickly defences, but their game of one-upmanship backfired and hurt them both. Annie always had to be top dog and if she went too far – which she did, biting off more than she could chew in the loan-shark business with Phil – it was to prove herself as good as any boy. George had always wanted a son, hence his obsession with Gianni, and Annie, knowing that, played rough. Unfortunately, the gang they crossed played rougher and Annie was beaten half to death. The experience hugely undermined her confidence and although she put on a brave front, she found it increasingly difficult to cope. Steve's rejection of her was the last straw and despite Annie regaining the upper hand (by selling her shares in the Health Club to Grant) it was a hollow victory, and she left.

A verbal Miss Whiplash, she tore strips off anyone who crossed her

Annie Palmer

Born 27.11.68

(Nadia Sawalha)

Melanie Healy

Born 15.01.72

(Tamzin Outhwaite)

Mel and Ian – could it ever have worked? Patently not. Mel is as free-spirited as Ian Beale is mean-spirited; she's exuberant, he's exasperating; she's a beauty, he's a beast. When she agreed to marry him, the question on everyone's lips was, why? OK, so Steve Owen was a two-timing, murdering, commitment-phobe, but at least that made him interesting! All Ian wanted was a cash-and-wrap bride he could show off in his shop. It was a long time before Mel cottoned on to this – she even chased all the way to Cornwall to make up with him – but by the time she'd come to her senses (on the pier at Brighton with seductive Steve Owen again), it was too late. Lucy was ill, Ian was desperate and Mel was trapped. After they'd tied the knot at the great Millennium double wedding, she discovered Ian had lied and ditched him on the spot. He tried buying her half the pub, but he could have offered her the moon for all the good it would have done him. She's now in her element behind the bar at the Vic with Dan Sullivan, another restless soul with a troubled past. We know Mel's got a troubled past because she told best friend Lisa. She's owned a business that went bankrupt, has been abused by a boyfriend, was estranged from her family and slept her way round the Greek islands, and that's just for starters. While she's made amends with father, Jeff, and brother, Alex, there's still more to come out about wild-at-heart Melanie. Count on it.

Jeff's been a rabid left-winger all his life and still likes to keep the red flag flying whenever he gets the chance – which isn't often these days, Albert Square not being a hotbed of political fervour. He was a print union steward in Fleet Street for 30 years and effectively alienated his wife, Jane, and three children, Katie, Alex and Melanie, with his opinionated attitude – when he was home, that was. Most of his time was spent attending to union business and he was always more comfortable with the political rather than the personal. Both Alex and Melanie rebelled against their father's domineering personality by getting in with bad crowds and then veering off on their own, very different paths, while Jane, sick of their sham of a marriage, found herself a more sympathetic bloke and left. By this time Jeff had been made redundant, shattering him completely, and it was a very bitter man who came to Walford to live with Alex, now a vicar. Given his history of relationships, Jeff isn't exactly cut out to be a Casanova, but he has set several female hearts fluttering in the Square. Dot,

Jeff Healy

Born 26.03.45

(Leslie Schofield)

egged on by Lilly, thought he had a thing for her and Rosa di Marco, who Jeff worked for as a waiter, has shown signs of regretting turning him down. However, it was pragmatic Pauline Fowler who struck lucky and, since their Christmas kiss, the couple have considered themselves an item. This is one union Jeff looks happy to be in and it's brought about a revolution all of its own: Pauline's wardrobe. Now that's got to be for the greater good of everybody.

SEE ALSO:
Kathy Mitchell, Sarah Hills, Ian Beale, Pauline Fowler, Steve Owen

Alex Healy

Alex's thoughts were less concerned with the heavenly host and more with Kathy's heavenly body

Born 03.07.67

(Richard Driscoll)

Sexy vicar Alex was always passionate about pastoral work – he set up a hostel for the homeless next to his church and instigated a halfway house for ex-offenders – but his downfall was to get rather too passionate about one particular member of his flock. After Kathy Mitchell left Phil she found herself increasingly drawn to Alex, who was understanding and easy to talk to. Meanwhile, Alex, at loggerheads with Kathy's son Ian over Bridge House, the rehabilitation centre, found her open-mindedness refreshing and a chord was struck. By Christmas Day 1997, Alex's thoughts were less concerned with the heavenly host and more with Kathy's heavenly body. They snogged in the vestry and if Peggy hadn't arrived with the Christmas puddings, Alex might have thrown caution and cassock to the wind. (As it was, that happened later.) The affair – which was discovered by Dot – sparked a massive crisis of faith for Alex and he was even prepared to abandon the priesthood, but Kathy refused to let him. She went to South Africa alone, leaving Alex broken-hearted. Jeff turning up on the vicarage doorstep did nothing to lift Alex's spirits – father and son had never seen eye-to-eye over politics and religion – but he was at least diverted from his depression by having to take in Dot and Lilly, made homeless by a fire. If their competitive squabbling wasn't enough to contend with, long-lost sister Mel wandered into Walford, upping the ante with Jeff and pairing off with smug Ian Beale. The Healys eventually settled their differences but by then Alex had lost his sense of purpose and was drifting. When the opportunity arrived to take his life in a new direction – working at a mission centre in Somalia – he took it.

Steve Owen

Born 1965
(Martin Kemp)

I s Steve Owen really the cad he's made out to be? Inscrutable Steve's always appeared ice cool, but his emotional revelations in the Vic about Saskia's death suggest that underneath his black leather exterior there beats a human heart. Possibly. Whether it's all an act or not (remember his 'impassioned' outburst in court?), he is capable of fear: since Matthew Rose's terror campaign, the cracks in Steve's charisma are becoming larger by the day. When he first arrived in the Square to run night spot E20 it soon became clear he was an arch manipulator, both in love and in business. He swept Mel her off her feet (almost literally) and sprang a seduction campaign on her that was working well until his ex-girlfriend, mad Saskia, started stirring. When Saskia went OTT on Valentine's Day, Steve lashed out in self-defence and killed her. The rest is history: he buried the body, forcing an unwilling Matthew *(above, right)* to be his accomplice, and when they were eventually caught, Steve got off while Matthew was left to rot in jail. It's hardly surprising the boy went bananas and held him hostage. Now Steve needs pills to make him sleep and although he's putting on a brave face for sister Jackie, he's beginning to lose control. Heavens, he slept with Sam Mitchell for safety! Not only that, he let soulmate Mel slip through his fingers. He'll start being nice to small children next (well, he was, actually, to Lucy). Villains ain't what they used to be...

When Saskia went OTT on Valentine's Day, Steve lashed out in self-defence and killed her

SEE ALSO:
Matthew Rose, Gianni di Marco

Jackie Owen

Born 15.08.63

(Race Davies)

There's something strange about Jackie. Maybe it's the bolshy way she juts her bottom lip out. Maybe it's the way she bites off sentences with her sharp white teeth. Maybe it's the way her body bristles and her eyes flash, even when she's ordering a dry white wine. Whatever it is, she's scarier than brother Steve. Poor Gianni di Marco, the lumbering, love-struck dolt. After years of playing the field, he has to fall for a vampire. OK, so far Jackie has only bitten his head off metaphorically, but you can see he's in for a rough ride. Jackie's got a temper, and when she loses it the signs are she really loses it. She keeps things pent up inside – her hatred of her mother, her hatred of herself, her hatred of the unjust world that took her beloved husband Doug from her. (Doug, a hotelier and club owner, committed suicide in prison when he was sent down for manslaughter after getting into a fight and killing his assailant in self-defence. Which, by amazing coincidence, is exactly what happened to Steve.) Jackie went into a sort of emotional suspended animation for five years until news of her brother's plight brought her to Walford. She got a job waitressing at Giuseppe's and it was

her moving testimony that probably bought Steve his freedom. Jackie and Gianni got together after the Arches collapsed on top of them and she is definitely the one wearing the trousers. She pushed him into making a play for the Vic and used her influence with the di Marcos to reintegrate Steve. All Jackie has to do is bare her teeth and Gianni comes running. He thinks she's smiling, of course.

Significant others

Saskia Duncan

Born 19.02.70 **Died** Feb 99

(Deborah Sheridan-Taylor)

Saskia wasn't in *EastEnders* for very long (unless you count the months she lay buried in Epping Forest) but her role was pivotal. She was an attractive but brittle blonde who had tagged onto Steve Owen after hanging out at his club. At first things were genuinely good between them, but as he became more distracted by financial problems at work, Saskia became increasingly jealous and needy. When she got pregnant, he insisted she get rid of the baby and Saskia, blinded by her feelings for him, let herself be persuaded. This tipped the balance, and as Steve grew colder and more remote, Saskia's preoccupation with him spilled over into madness. One day Steve sold his club and left, without telling Saskia, and she spent the next few months obsessively trying to track him down. When we first saw her in the Square she was scoring the paintwork on Steve's BMW with a funny gleam in her eye. It didn't stop there. She stalked Steve, seduced him into sleeping with her again, then told Mel, who ditched him. Happy to have cleared the field, Saskia assumed Steve would take her back and was furious when he refused. She talked her way into his office on Valentine's Day, flew at him in a rage and tried to kill him. She might well have succeeded if Steve hadn't brained her with an ashtray. As it was, she ended up in a bin bag, a sorry end to a wasted life.

Finding out his doctor flatmate was homosexual came as a shock

Mick McFarlane

Born 04.04.68

(Sylvester Williams)

Mick is an accomplished keyboard player and loves jazz. He has formed several, not very successful bands, which was how he met singer Frankie (who went on to seduce Alan Jackson). Frankie was followed by another female soloist, Lola, who Mick also fell for. They started dating but she was always rushing off without warning, and he was shocked to discover she had a young son. Lola got her own recording contract and left the band and Mick's life, and he's steered clear of women until recently, when things started warming up nicely between him and Nina. Money's frequently a problem for Mick, especially now he's playing surrogate dad to half-sister Kim. He managed the night café until it was closed down by a bout of food poisoning (not his fault) and now runs the music stall, having bought out Matthew Rose with a loan from lodger Fred Fonseca *(above, right)*. Finding out his doctor flatmate was homosexual came as a shock to Mick, who remained blithely ignorant even when Fred took him to a gay ball in Brighton. When he found out the truth, Mick was outraged at Fred's lack of trust in him – and just as perturbed to discover Fred didn't fancy him! There's no pleasing some men!

Josie McFarlane

Born 1945
(Joan Hooley)

Pretty schoolgirl Kim is the product of an affair Mick's father had when he was temporarily estranged from Josie. Her mother died when she was 8 and Josie – who had lost her husband by then, too – adopted Kim, rather than see her taken into care. When she brought her to Walford from Jamaica, Josie initially presented Kim as Mick's cousin, before telling him the truth. Mick, not the judgemental type, was cool about it, although he found Kim's tagging round after him a little irksome at first. Since then, Kim has slotted in well to life at Walford High School and has befriended Sonia and Nicky. After attending a modelling audition with Nicky – to give her moral support – it was Kim who was picked, delighting ambitious Josie. Kim was subsequently rejected at a casting for not being slim enough and started cutting out food, developing an eating disorder that threatened to spiral dangerously out of control. It took the combined efforts of Mick and Dr Fred Fonseca to get Kim back on the road to recovery. It's been a confusing time for the insecure teenager, especially with Josie being forced to leave the country, but with her big brother's help she may be able to put down roots at last.

Josie always looked a pretty together woman, but her well-groomed appearance and confident manner was a front that masked a lifetime of setbacks and disappointments. Josie set high – if not impossible – standards, and inevitably people failed her: the husband she had worshipped died, leaving her his illegitimate child; her son was going to be a professional musician and ended up selling CDs on a stall; her employer was an irreproachable physician who turned out to be gay. But what was hardest for Josie to admit was that she'd failed herself. The McFarlanes had been defrauded in a Jamaican property scam and when she and Kim arrived on Mick's doorstep, Josie was practically penniless. She eventually made a new life for herself in Albert Square, proving herself a competent barmaid and later becoming Dr Fred Fonseca's receptionist. After a bumpy initiation, in which a ferociously protective Josie scared off most of the patients, things settled down, but Josie couldn't cope with the revelation about Fred's sexuality. She claimed that working for him conflicted with her religious beliefs, suspected Fred of 'recruiting' Kim to the gay cause and accused Mick of associating with 'undesirables' (including ex-prostitute Nina, a fallen woman in Josie's book). It took bigoted remarks by racist Jim Branning to make Josie realise she was as prejudiced in her own way as he was, but by then it was too late. Having forgotten to renew her visa, she was threatened with deportation and returned to Jamaica minus Kim, with Mick's warning about her becoming a lonely, bitter old woman ringing in her ears.

Kim McFarlane

Born 05.08.86
(Krystle Williams)

Three cheers for Dot Cotton! She's a ghoul and a gossip and smokes like a chimney, but *EastEnders* just wouldn't be the same without Dot's burgundy barnet and stare of slack-jawed disbelief as she witnesses yet another moral outrage from her post at the launderette: 'Ooh, I say, Pauline...' Dot's principally a comic character, but although her role tends towards leading a Greek (make that cockney) chorus with Pauline and Ethel *(right)*, there's been plenty of pathos and not a bit of high drama in her life. Almost all of this has centred round her Nick, Dot's only son, although Charlie, her bigamist late husband, gave her his fair share of grief. Nick's an out-and-out blackhearted villain and in the end even Dot, a religious woman with a strong mothering streak, gave up and turned him over to the police. It took many years before the scales finally fell from her eyes, though: Nick murdered and stole, pimped and poisoned, conned and threatened, blackmailed and bullied, produced fake grandchildren, fake drugs prescriptions and fake beliefs, all to

squeeze money out of his old ma. He did also produce one real grandchild, Ashley, and Dot even lived with Nick and his girlfriend Zoe in Essex for a while, but predictably this didn't work out. For a woman of such zeal, Dot is surprisingly tolerant and has given shelter and support to a number of waifs and strays, including Donna, Rod, Hazel, Disa and Nigel, who became virtually a replacement son. She's been more understanding about Mark's HIV than supposedly liberal-minded Lilly *(below, left)*, and since moving in at the Fowlers' has even shown sympathy for noxious Martin. Which is almost beyond the call of duty for anyone.

Dot Cotton

Born 1936

(June Brown)

EastEnders just wouldn't be the same without Dot's burgundy barnet

Nick Cotton

Born 1959
(John Altman)

Nick Cotton was responsible for *EastEnders'* opening scandal back in the very first episode in 1985: the murder of old Reg Cox. His behaviour did not improve thereafter. He was a heroin addict and a racist and a thoroughly nasty piece of work who exploited and abused anyone he could and had no qualms about killing anyone who stood in his way. Nick was responsible for the murder of Eddie Royle – which he tried to set up Clyde Tavernier for – and almost succeeded in poisoning his own mother, Dot, to get his hands on her bingo winnings. However, even he couldn't go through with it, this being the one and only shred of decency he's ever exhibited. He messed with Dot's mind terribly and each time he reappeared in the Square looking more dishevelled and dirty and desperate you knew he'd try and con her again, and you knew she'd fall for it, too. For many years, Dot couldn't face up to the truth about her son and blamed herself for indulging him when he was little. But Nick's amorality was in his genes (undoubtedly from his father Charlie's side) and Dot finally acknowledged this and stopped making excuses for him. Nick's relationships with women – when he wasn't pimping or beating them – were transitory, but he did enjoy a short spell of domesticity with Zoe, fathering a son, Ashley *(right)*, before prison, Nick's second home, reclaimed him on yet another drug-related offence. He is currently doing another long stretch at Her Majesty's Pleasure after Dot shopped him to the Old Bill, so it seems unlikely he'll return to the Square. Then again, never say never.

A thoroughly nasty piece of work

Charlie, Dot's late husband, was a sly, shifty, weaselly man and not the saint she paints him as at all. Time has obviously bestowed upon Charlie an unnatural gloss in Dot's memory: their wedding was 44 years ago, after all, and he only stayed with her for two years after that, so it's bound to be a bit hazy. Still, even Dot can't kid herself about the basic facts. Charlie deserted her when she was pregnant with Nick (having forced her to terminate

Charlie Cotton

Born 1931 **Died** Jul 91

(Christopher Hancock)

an earlier pregnancy) and she was left to bring their child up alone. True, Charlie reappeared occasionally – usually when he wanted money or temporary accommodation – but he always sloped off again, leaving her with an empty wallet to soldier on alone. She also had to bear the humiliation of knowing that Charlie, a long-distance lorry driver, had another other woman in his life, her half-sister Rose, who lived in Liverpool. To add insult to injury, Charlie had a bigamous marriage to a woman called Joan, who knew him as Tommy. This came to light when Joan came to Walford looking for him and met Dot. They cornered Charlie, who fessed up and fled, though he did buy Dot a new gas cooker by way of compensation. Charlie tried appealing to Nick's better nature (!) over the poisoning (although it was Dot calling Nick's bluff that ultimately stopped him), and he did expose the fake grandchild scam, so perhaps he did have one or two mildly redeeming features. He was killed in a motorway crash in his lorry in 1991 and, frankly, no-one's missed him. Not even, if truth be told, Dot.

You couldn't really let a man like Dan Sullivan go for long. He's way too gorgeous. Women the length and breadth of the country were fantasising about being in Bianca's shoes and when Dan and Bianca's passionate affair ended in tears all round, it wasn't just B who we gave a misty-eyed send-off to at Euston. OK, so what Dan did was disgraceful, but he still managed to be a sympathetic character, mainly because he couldn't help himself. He was weak, he was stupid and he was reckless, but he wasn't innately bad. He was just a bloke. Foolhardy, fallible and all too recognisable. When Dan returned to the Square in December 1999, it was clear the time away hadn't served him well. He was down on his uppers having been on a massive bender for three months, neglecting his business (he works in the rag trade) and, as a consequence, losing his flat and all his money. Phil, the only person to stick by him before, took him in and then made Dan's Christmas by selling him half of the Vic (signed over to Phil by Grant) for a fiver. This was throwing down the gauntlet to an apoplectic Peggy and Frank, who Phil was at war with, although Dan had no particular axe to grind and simply wanted to make something of himself again. Farcical scenes behind the bar ensued, but by all accounts, Dan is now pulling in the (female) punters and has won round many of the regulars – except Ricky – although he's still in dire straits financially and is resorting to dodgy means (eg lock-ins) to get by. He's also proving to make a good team with Mel. Now wouldn't those two make a lovely couple?

Dan Sullivan

Born 1967
(Craig Fairbrass)

Lisa Shaw

Born 28.06.68
(Lucy Benjamin)

She was reduced to throwing herself at Gianni di Marco to prove her desirability

Lovely Lisa came to Walford as the assistant market inspector and was soon taking her job description a little too literally, providing back-up for her boss, Michael Rose, after hours too when his wife was away. Having lost her virginity to middle-aged Michael, Lisa, then 30 (she was a very late starter), assumed this was the Real Thing and planned a blissful future sorting out stalls together, but it was not to be. She was reduced to throwing herself at Gianni di Marco to prove her desirability, who thought all his birthdays had come at once, but after dragging him back to her place Lisa froze him out (she did sleep with him later, thinking that made him her boyfriend, and Gianni promptly disillusioned her). Mark Fowler, a biker like Lisa, proved a staunch ally throughout this crisis of confidence and offered her a room in

Nina, Irene Raymond's niece, arrived in the Square with a big secret: she's an ex-prostitute. Having fitted up her violent pimp, Vinny, a boyfriend who had got her hooked on drugs before persuading her to go on the game to feed his own habit, Nina left the

Harris
Nina

Born 16.11.72

(Troy Titus-Adams)

his house, although his motives were never entirely pure. Having overheard Lisa tell Jamie – who she took under her wing – that she'd nursed her mother through terminal cancer, he felt unable to confess his feelings for her and watched with growing dismay as she latched onto Phil Mitchell. (Why? Why?) Encouraged by Mel, Lisa's best mate and confidante, Mark eventually poured out his love to Lisa, only to be knocked back with the old 'let's just be friends' routine. However, since then Phil's shown what he's made of by rejecting Lisa when she found out she was pregnant – and it wasn't just because she wouldn't fit into her leathers – and good old Mark has stepped into the breach. Will Lisa realise what she's got under her nose? Will Mark live to help her bring up the baby? Will Phil change his mind? This one will run and run …

lifestyle behind and cleaned up her act. With Vinny safely locked away, her determination to start afresh led her to consider social work as an option, something she'd had a great deal of experience of, having been in care as a child after her mother (Irene's sister, Jenny) neglected her. She is currently studying to get on the relevant training course and works in the Vic to support herself. Even though she wasn't very good behind the bar to start with, Peggy took her on because she was an attractive girl who brightened up the place. Nina was sympathetic towards Grant, who had just lost Tiffany, and provided a shoulder for him to cry on, a relationship that eventually blossomed into hearts and flowers and fluffy bunnies. This did not last long: Dean, a former punter who was blackmailing Nina, informed Grant of

her less-than-perfect past and Grant went from Caring Guy to Raving Loony in two seconds flat and broadcast the news to the entire pub. Beppe, who used to be a Vice cop and had known many girls like Nina, befriended her and rented her a room in his flat, and it was his support that persuaded her to stay and front it out. Their friendship is strictly platonic (although Sam was jealous of their closeness) and Nina is now seeing Mick. It's a slow-burn relationship, but who knows? She likes his taste in music, and that's always a good start.

Ethel Skinner

Born 19.02.16

(Gretchen Franklin)

She was famous for her (questionable) ability to read palms and tea-leaves

Ethel Skinner's 84 years old, remembers trams, lived through the Blitz and is fond of reminiscing about the gay times she had with GIs. Ethel's memory, never very dependable, has tended to filter out the bad bits: in fact, she wafted through the war on a wave of sedatives and booze after the shock of having her entire family wiped out by a doodlebug sent her slightly loopy. She began dressing outrageously, wearing garish makeup, flirting and knocking back gin – traits that have lasted to this day – and was almost a permanent fixture at the Vic with her orange wig, false teeth, teacosy hats and pug dog. Willy, Ethel's pug (she named him after her late husband) was always tucked under her arm and she loved him dearly, so it was a dark day indeed when he had to be put down, and Ethel was quite heartbroken. She was famous for her (questionable) ability to read palms and tea-leaves and once earned a living from it, but she was equally famous for her hilarious malapropisms. For years Ethel was a comic double act with Dot, and although the two used to spar constantly they depended on each other. Ethel may have seemed a bit barmy, but she has always been the more astute – she realised Nick was poisoning Dot – and has always had more success with men, to Dot's disgust. She's had several boyfriends, including Benny Bloom, a friend of Dr Legg, who she got engaged to (sadly, he died, though he did leave her £2,000) and Reggie, who she met at a tea dance. These days we see little of Ethel as she's become very frail and lives in sheltered accommodation some way from the Square.

Martin Fowler's mate, Asif moved to Walford fairly recently when his parents bought the mini-mart in Walford High Street. He's a Muslim, born in Whitechapel, and his family hails from Kashmir. Like Martin he's a troublemaker, although Asif's behaviour stems more from a desire to impress and he tends to make himself scarce when it all blows up. It was Asif who dared Martin to nick the cash in Giuseppe's, causing Jackie and Gianni to chase him into the Arches, which then collapsed on top of them. Asif and Martin were also responsible for trashing Steve Owen's car, and when Steve discovered that Asif had a record for breaking into a neighbour's car, he collared him and forced him to confess. He hasn't exactly endeared himself to girls so far, either. He dated Nicky di Marco but bragged that they'd gone farther than they had, and is fond of making uncheckable claims, eg that he's snogged a cousin in Kashmir (he hasn't). He has a crush on Janine, who he (correctly) views as experienced and a goer, but she is way out of his league and has made this crystal clear to him.

Not much is known about Marcus Christie. He's a tight-lipped, balding, bespectacled solicitor in his mid-50's who the Mitchell family have retained over the years and who Grant tended to shout at a lot on the phone. Christie is a formal man who speaks clipped, precise English, sports a bow tie and has an office full of leather-bound volumes. He doesn't look like the archetypal bent brief, but it is precisely his ability to, shall we say,

Marcus Christie

Born not known
(Stephen Churchett)

Asif Malik

Born 09.84
(Ashvin Luximon)

'circumvent' legal problems that has kept him in with the Mitchells. Phil went to Marcus Christie when he was caught dealing in stolen motors (he got off and Ricky, *right*, carried the can) and both times Grant wound up in prison, Marcus Christie acted as his solicitor. He provided dodgy forms when the bruvs tried to get Ricky sectioned to stop him absconding with Sam, and has also been on hand for divorces and custody battles. It was Christie who put the idea into Grant's head about trying to prove Tiffany an unfit mother, although he did tell Ricky not to bother fighting Bianca for custody of Liam. Even with Grant off the scene, given the Mitchells' track record, Marcus Christie is sure to pop up again. Unless he's replaced with a stuffed shirt, that is!

blasts from the past

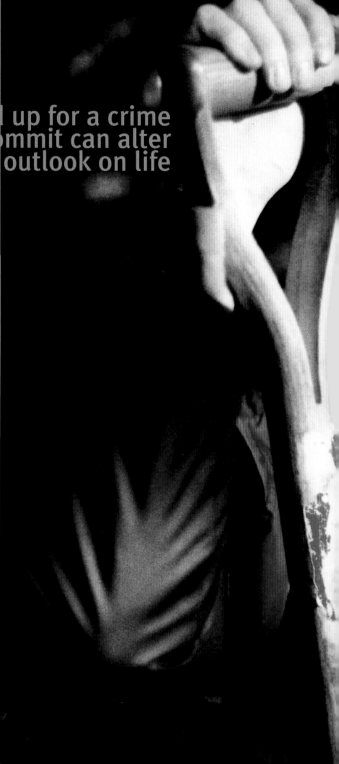

Being banged up for a crime you didn't commit can alter your outlook on life

Fred Fonseca

Arrived in the Square Jan 99 **Left** Feb 2000

(Jimi Mistry)

Fred Fonseca, Dr Legg's replacement, was young, good-looking and gay. No-one, including his flatmate, Mick, knew the last bit until just before he left (he came out on a wild weekend in Brighton). Up until then he was more notorious for his brusque bedside manner. Since he had apparently been celibate the entire 18 months he spent in the Square, perhaps that explains it.

Matthew Rose

Arrived in the Square Aug 97 **Left** Feb 2000

(Joe Absolom)

Mad Matt started off as such a nice boy. OK, so he tried it on a bit – getting engaged to Sarah Hills just so that he could have sex was definitely beyond the pale, and he shouldn't have stitched up Lenny and Huw over DJ-ing at E20 – but barring these machine-washable stains on his character, young Matthew certainly seemed harmless enough. So how did he end up as a slavering psychotic? Being banged up for a crime you didn't commit can alter your outlook on life, and Matthew's was changed irrevocably after he was found guilty of the manslaughter of Saskia Duncan. In fact, Matthew witnessed Steve Owen (*inset, left*) kill Saskia and was forced to help him dispose of her body and then pressured into keeping his mouth shut. They were both subsequently arrested, each blaming the other for striking the fatal blow, and after a hairy time on remand, in which pretty-boy Matthew got more male attention than he'd bargained for, the jury found him guilty and Steve walked free. Understandably, Matthew had plenty of time for brooding after that and when the murder weapon was recovered with Steve's prints on it, Matthew was released and planned his retribution. He conducted a campaign of terror against Steve which culminated in him holding Steve hostage in his office. After videoing Steve's pleading and grovelling (presumably to play over and over to himself in a darkened room, grinning manically), Matthew sloped off into the night and was never seen again.

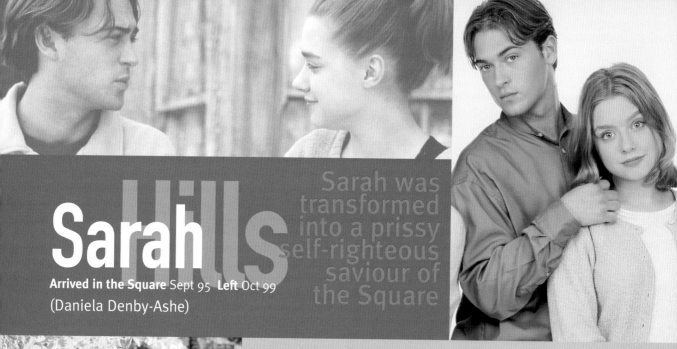

Sarah Hills

Arrived in the Square Sept 95 **Left** Oct 99
(Daniela Denby-Ashe)

Sarah was transformed into a prissy self-righteous saviour of the Square

When Sarah first came to Albert Square she was a naive, mixed-up kid who shoplifted to get attention and latched on to anyone who showed an interest in her. Alastair, the leader of the Walford Christian Fellowship, spotted her vulnerability and befriended her, and suddenly Sarah's life had a whole new focus: religion. Overnight, Sarah was transformed into a prissy, self-righteous saviour of the Square, becoming so fervent that even when her drink was spiked with Ecstasy (at Blackpool) she thought her 'trip' was a mission from God. It was only when Sarah discovered that hypocrite Alastair was sleeping with his girlfriend (having preached that sex before marriage was a cardinal sin) that the scales fell from her eyes. Having previously refused to do it with her boyfriend, Joe Wicks (*above*), she collared Robbie Jackson, seduced him on the sofa, then ran off in a state and experienced a brief, tortured spell in the wilderness – ie on the streets – before meeting Walford vicar Alex Healy, who gave her a different perspective on faith. She remained a do-gooder, helping out at Alex's shelter and teaching reading to an illiterate ex-offender, but despite her earnestness she frequently got things wrong and upset people. Her love life was never that great: she got engaged to Joe but he went back to Bolton; she got engaged to Matthew but it was a trick to get her into bed; Luca, a friend of Teresa's, seemed OK until he tried to force her to have sex with him, and the less said about Robbie's fateful pizza delivery, the better. By the time she left though, (to go to University), she had acquired a glimmer of a sense of humour and her parting shot, stitching up sleazeball Gianni at a party, was a hilarious masterstroke.

Lenny Wallace

Arrived in the Square May 96 **Left** Jul 99

(Desune Coleman)

Barman Lenny was a happy-go-lucky charmer who liked an easy life and couldn't commit to women, jobs or mortgages. He lived in the squat with sidekick Huw and they shared a common interest in loud music, winding up Ian Beale and getting off with girls. Sexy Lenny was much more successful at this – he slept with Bianca and Teresa – but his past caught up with him when he discovered he might have contracted hepatitis B through his promiscuity.

Huw Edwards

Arrived in the Square May 96 **Left** Apr 99

(Richard Elis)

Stocky, amiable Welshman Huw had a dry sense of humour and a vaguely philosophical bent (usually after a few pints). He worked in George Palmer's club with Lenny, then in the café, but no-one knew about Huw's real talent – art – until he launched into an unbidden treatise on abstraction at an exhibition in the café. The artist, Carrie, a babe traditionally out of his league, was so impressed that she went off with Huw to help him find himself.

Lilly Mattock

Arrived in the Square Nov 98 **Left** Sept 99

(Barbara Keogh)

Dot's sometime companion Lilly (though they were chalk and cheese), was a former hoofer with the Westwood Girls, and never let anyone forget it. She was clearly a bit wild for Walford, trouncing Huw and Lenny at poker and joining in salsa classes, and had to be barred from clubbing at E20 for fear of upstaging Steve's younger clientele. She was a bit of a stirrer, encouraging Dot ('Dorothy', as she always called her) to think that Jeff Healy had amorous intentions towards her, getting Dot all of a fluster. Lilly moved on when the insurance cheque for her flat came through and Dot went to stay with Pauline.

Troy Harvey

He turned out to be a serial-older-womaniser

Arrived in the Square Sep 99 **Left** Dec 99

(Jamie Jarvis)

Free spirit Troy was backpacking through London when he dropped in to see his old mate Tony Hills and ended up seducing Tony's old mum, Irene *(right)* instead. Irene did her best to resist, but Troy's intense stare and snake hips proved too much for her resolve and soon they were at it everywhere. He turned out to be a serial-older-womaniser and subsequently made a pass at Rosa before being booted out by an angry Terry.

Tony Hills

He was confused about his sexuality and as they say, swung both ways

Arrived in the Square Sept 95 **Left** Apr 99

(Mark Homer)

Tony started off as a smalltime drug-dealer and general waster and progressed to campaigning journalist and Purveyor of the Truth, although this didn't serve him very much better. He finally renounced drugs after the Blackpool incident with Sarah *(above, left)* and, after a long period of lying on the sofa, got a job as a dogsbody on the *Walford Gazette*. Having impressed the editor, Max, by landing a scoop in-between photocopying and making the tea, Tony was promoted to trainee, but bit off more than he could chew when he investigated a corrupt councillor's relationship with crime boss George Palmer. Max refused to run it after Annie Palmer nobbled him and Tony got the sack for his efforts. He was confused about his sexuality and, as they say, swung both ways, initially sleeping with Tiffany (who thought he might have been the father of her child – he wasn't) before settling for her gay brother Simon. Fortunately, the three of them came to an amicable arrangement about this, but the domestic bliss was short-lived. Tony started having affairs with women, including man-eater Frankie (who went all bunny-boiler on him,

serving him right) and then peroxide hackette Polly *(above, right)*, a betrayal surely all the more bitter because only a truly desperate man could have slept with a hairstyle like hers. Simon walked out and Tony subsequently dallied half-heartedly with Teresa di Marco whilst yearning secretly after his former boyfriend. Tony and Simon stole an illicit kiss on a riverbank in Norfolk, but didn't actually get back together until Tony left the Square to go travelling round Europe, prompting dithering Simon to realise that he'd always wanted to go grape-picking and join him.

Ratty Susan had MS, so you could hardly blame her for being bitter, but it took a determined person to penetrate her aggressive front. Irene Hills managed it and, ironically, Lisa, but Susan rarely gave ex-husband Michael the time of day and the more her condition deteriorated, the nastier she was to him. Michael, emotionally locked out, took solace in Lisa's arms, although he did stick by Susan eventually.

Market inspector Michael was pudgy and greying but despite his unprepossessing appearance he had a remarkable allure for women with low self-esteem (April Branning, Lisa Shaw). He was a poor husband to ratty Susan and an inadequate dad to mad Matthew, but somehow you always felt sorry for him. How did he do that?

Susan&MichaelRose

Arrived in the Square Aug 97
Left Feb 99
(Tilly Vosburgh)

Arrived in the Square Feb 96
Left Oct 99
(Russell Floyd)

You could hardly blame her for being bitter

Conor, Pauline Fowler's Irish nephew, was a charming rogue with wild hair, dancing eyes and a way with the blarney, though he had a harder side, too, and lent muscle to Phil and Annie's debt-collecting. He was a natural flirt and notoriously irresponsible, constantly letting daughter Mary down, but after fathering a child with Ruth Fowler he belatedly turned over a new leaf. Oh, yeah...

Conor&Mary Flaherty

Arrived in the Square Sep 97 **Left** Feb 99

(Melanie Clark Pullen)

Arrived in the Square Sep 97 **Left** Feb 99

(Sean Gleeson)

She spoke her mind and quickly riled Tiffany when she started working at the Vic

Mary was a smart, pert, spirited lass who came to live with her Auntie Pauline after being whisked away from her violent Irish grandfather by the Fowlers. She spoke her mind and quickly riled Tiffany when she started working at the Vic, but was basically kind and sunny-tempered. She slept with Joe Wicks and was upset when he left, preferring to hang out in a crowd thereafter with Matt, Huw and Lenny.

iny Gita had the tenacity of a terrier and a bark quite as bad as her bite, something that her husband, easy-going Sanjay, always tried to steer well clear of. Gita was always the brains behind the business – they owned a clothes stall in Bridge Street market – and Sanjay was the impulsive one with the big schemes that never came off. He also had a weakness for gambling and women and couldn't be trusted around betting shops or pretty faces, although Gita wasn't exactly faithful either. After Sanjay had an affair with her sister, Meena, Gita met smooth-talking Guppy while Sanjay was in India. Guppy not only romanced her but stung the Kapoors for £2,000 – and all the time he was in cahoots with Meena! Sanjay and Gita tried to get the trust back into their marriage by having another baby (they already had a daughter, Sharmilla), but had problems conceiving and eventually discovered – to Sanjay's chagrin – that he had a low sperm count. To make matters worse, Sanjay's mother, Neelam, turned up on the doorstep and immediately started interfering. IVF treatment failed, and soon after, Gita disappeared mysteriously with Sharmilla, sending

Sanjay&Gita

Arrived in the Square Feb 93
Left Sep 98
(Deepak Verma)

Arrived in the Square Feb
Left Sep 98
(Shobu Kapoor)

everyone into a spin. Wild theories were expounded and Sanjay was arrested for her attempted murder (he was later released due to lack of evidence). No-one was sure if he was really innocent or not until Ruth tracked down Gita to a hospital, where she had just given birth to another man's child (the product of a one-night stand). Sanjay took her back and agreed to accept the baby as his own, but they were forced to flee the Square after the tabloids got hold of the scandal and set up camp on their doorstep.

Meena McKenzie

Arrived in the Square Jul 93 **Left** Jan 96

(Sudha Bhuchar)

Kapoor

Gita was always the brains behind the business ...

Sanjay was the impulsive one with the big schemes that never came off

Meena *(above, left)* was the sister from hell, first bossing Gita about, then stealing her husband, Sanjay, and finally, after Gita had refused to see her ever again, fixing up for her fiancé, Guppy, to approach Gita with a business deal, hoping this would bring her sister round. This backfired when he and Gita fell for each other (although they didn't sleep together). After the inevitable sibling showdown Gita and Meena never spoke again, and Meena lost her man into the bargain.

Kapoor Neelam

Arrived in the Square Mar 97 **Left** Jul 98

(Jamila Massey)

She was hard-bitten, cynical, ambitious and never allowed sentiment to get in the way

Sanjay's mother was a formidable woman with traditional views who often clashed with her Westernised daughter-in-law, Gita. When she came to Walford, she was shocked to discover that her son's 'fashion emporium' was merely a market stall, but pitched in nonetheless. Neelam bought the First 'til Last and ran it for a while, but she could not condone Sanjay taking on another man's baby and left, disowning the lot of them.

Polly Becker

Arrived in the Square May 97 **Left** Sep 98

(Victoria Gould)

Polly – an investigative journalist on the *Walford Gazette* who befriended and even slept with Tony Hills – was hard-bitten, cynical, ambitious and never allowed sentiment to get in the way of a good story (it was Polly who sold the Kapoors' story to the nationals by exploiting her friendship with Ruth). And if her character seemed cliched, well – that's what a lot of hacks are like, only most of them can find their way to a decent hairdresser, eventually.

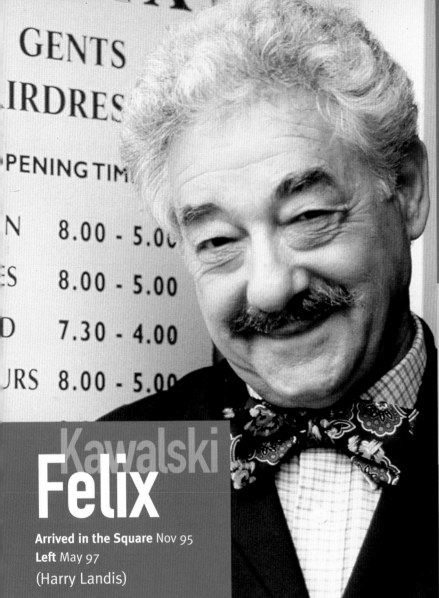

GENTS
IRDRES

PENING TIM

N   8.00 - 5.00
ES   8.00 - 5.00
D   7.30 - 4.00
URS 8.00 - 5.00

Felix Kawalski

Arrived in the Square Nov 95
Left May 97

(Harry Landis)

F elix was a sweet little inoffensive Polish man who set up a barber's shop in Walford and somehow got the reputation of being a wife-murdering pervert who had buried his missus under the floorboards. His mysterious cellar eventually proved to contain only his prized butterfly collection, but not before a posse from the Vic almost flattened the old boy, assuming he'd attacked Clare. Felix lasted a year before leaving to trace relatives in Israel, presumably on the basis that he'd have a quieter life there...

T ed, Kathy's brother, was an overbearing, insensitive oaf who came on the heavy-handed Victorian father to his children, Tony and Sarah. Too heavy-handed as it turned out: he nearly did for Robbie Jackson after finding out he'd slept with Sarah. He was as hopeless with money as he was with relationships, and after his hardware shop went bust he went off to work on building projects in Dubai and then South Africa, which is where Kathy met up with him again.

Ted Hills

Arrived in the Square Aug 85 **Left** Aug 97

(Brian Croucher)

Nigel Bates

He had the world's worst taste in shirts and ties

Arrived in the Square Mar 92 **Left** Apr 98

(Paul Bradley)

Nigel was a lovely, lovely man with two flaws: his inability to say 'no' to a fry-up and his faith in Grant Mitchell. Nigel and Grant's friendship went back to their schooldays, though what had brought or kept these two diametrically opposed personalities together wasn't quite clear. Nigel was a true mate and stuck by Grant through times when no-one else would, notably after Sharongate. (Grant later repaid this loyalty by waltzing off with Lorraine, the girl Nigel was in love with, despite knowing how he felt about her.) Nigel's other enduring friendship was with Dot Cotton, his former landlady, who mothered him rotten and who he looked out for in return when Nick turned up to cause trouble. Nigel was overweight, shy, had the world's worst taste in shirts and ties and sported a mop of shaggy curls reminiscent of 70's footballers, so it wasn't often he found success with the opposite sex, although women were drawn to his gentleness and humour more than he realised. He was bowled over when Debbie, a single mum with a daughter, Clare, agreed to go out with him, and even more ecstatic when she married him in July 1994 – with a few hiccups concerning her violent ex, Liam *(left)*, although Grant came into his own here and sorted the bloke out. Their happiness was short-lived: Debs was killed in a road accident the following year and, on top of his grief, Nigel was faced with a custody battle for Clare, instigated by Liam. Nigel won and he and Clare got on with their lives, supporting each other, but it was three years before he met anyone special enough to take Debs's place – Clare's teacher, Julie Haye *(far right)* – and was able to let go of the past.

At one point her strength of character spilled over into bullying

Clare, Debs's daughter, adored Nigel and was often more adult about things than he was, particularly after Debs died. At one point her strength of character spilled over into bullying and Nigel took her back to his old school to make a point about the misery bullies inflict, which struck home. She later met a boy, Josh, who conveniently turned out to be Julie Haye's son, and they all moved up to Scotland together.

Clare Bates

Arrived in the Square Jul 93 **Left** Apr 98

(Gemma Bissix)

Debbie Bates

Arrived in the Square May 93 **Died** Jun 95

(Nicola Duffett)

Blonde Debs didn't commit to Nigel straight away because of husband Liam, who she kept going back to out of guilt about Clare. When she and Nigel finally tied the knot – marked by a street party for the entire Square – they were the world's happiest couple, a situation no storyliner worth their salt can allow for long. Poor Debs was sexually harassed by her boss at the bookies and then killed in a hit-and-run, but she did have a rosebush in the gardens planted in her name.

They were the world's happiest couple

Alistair Matthews

Arrived in the Square Apr 96 **Left** Mar 97

(Neil Clark)

Alistair was a creepy and manipulative evangelist, cunningly disguised as an innocuous department-store sales manager. Vulnerable Sarah Hills fell under his spell when he sucked her into the Walford Christian Fellowship. Alistair, however, did not practise the piety he preached and when Sarah found out about his pre-marital sinning with girlfriend Sue, she denounced him publicly, although he still managed to wriggle off the hook in front of his congregation.

Frankie Pierre

Arrived in the Square Jun 96 **Left** Mar 97

(Syan Blake)

Frankie had a
carnivorous approach
to relationships

Frankie had a carnivorous approach to relationships, hunting down her quarry, devouring her victim in two gulps and then moving on to the next kill. Alan Jackson got this treatment after Frankie, a singer with Mick's band, met him at a gig in the Night Café and dragged him back to her lair at Huw and Lenny's (*above*). She later sunk her fangs into Tony Hills but he chucked her first, stinging wacko Frankie into stalking him obsessively. Her scatter-gun approach to relationships finally misfired when she made a pass at evangelist Alastair Matthews, who turned her down, effectively crushing her ego.

Beetle-browed Dr Legg *(below, with Pauline Fowler)* was never at the cutting edge of medicine, but he was reliable and had a reassuring bedside manner – something that other incumbents, including his nephew and partner in the practice, Dr David Samuels (and later Fred Fonseca) failed notably to deliver. The one time he did fall down, failing to diagnose Vicki Fowler as having meningitis, he retired the same day, but he returned to work three months later and sacked David after complaints from the residents. He is now enjoying his retirement to the full.

Doctor Harold Legg

Arrived in the Square Feb 85 **Left** Feb 97
(Leonard Fenton)

Nellie Ellis

Arrived in the Square Dec 93 **Left** Mar 98
(Elizabeth Kelly)

Visiting 'Auntie Nellie' provides a regular excuse for Pauline to pop away from Albert Square, although she did appear in person for over a year (1994–95). When stingy Nellie wasn't giving Arthur grief, she was flirting in a buttoned-up sort of way with Jules Tavernier, and even moved in with him for a bit – although she made him sleep on the sofa. The Fowlers were relieved to see the back of the interfering old busybody when she finally got rehoused, and so, frankly, was every one else.

> Dr Legg was never at the cutting edge of medicine

Steve Elliot

Arrived in the Square Oct 91 **Left** Feb 96

(Mark Monero)

Chef Steve was a caterer, a ship's cook, a barman, a hairdresser and a café proprietor respectively and a bit of a dilettante where women were concerned, too. When girlfriend Hattie Tavernier proposed to him he ran off to sea rather than go through with the marriage, and he dumped Della and her hairdressing salon when he found out she was gay. Steve stole away with a girl called Lydia – a major commitment for him – but then they did have mobsters on their tail...

Geoff Barnes

Arrived in the Square May 94 **Left** Oct 95

(David Roper)

Portly, middle-aged Geoff was Michelle Fowler's tutor at university and, in the best *Educating Rita* tradition, helped her with her work and then got extra-curricular with her. Geoff was nice but unexciting and the age gap showed – he got on better with Pat! He and Chelle were due to marry, but Geoff nobly called it off knowing her heart wasn't in it. He ruined the effect by changing his mind, but by then Chelle was bound for America.

His hulking figure commanded respect

Big Ron

Big Ron

Arrived in the Square Feb 85 **Left** Feb 98

(Ron Tarr)

Gentle giant Ron was a presence in Albert Square right from the start. Famously, he hardly said anything in the 13 years he spent running his hardware stall and propping up the bar in the Vic, but his hulking figure commanded respect and he did a good line in menacing looks (as Robbie found out when he dated his daughter, Tina). Ron had a heart attack in 1993 but recovered and eventually left Walford in style, moving to Spain after becoming a lottery millionaire.

Impatient Laurie didn't even get past first base with Kathy

Laurie Bates

Arrived in the Square Sep 89 **Left** Mar 90

(Gary Powell)

Market trader Laurie queered Pete Beale's pitch in more ways than one: not only did he set up his fruit and veg stall in direct competition to the Beale family's long-established and never-disputed stall, sparking a cauliflowers-at-30-paces trade war, but he also went out with Pete's recently-ex wife, Kathy. There was really no need for Pete to gnash his teeth, though. After her rape (by Willmott-Brown), Kathy wasn't up for a full-on relationship and an impatient Laurie didn't even get past first base before she dropped him.

Shelley Lewis

Arrived in the Square Nov 92 **Left** Mar 94

(Nicole Arumugam)

Shelley, Michelle's college mate and lodger, was a user. She initially set her sights on Tricky Dicky, thinking he'd be a good meal ticket, but he sussed her and she moved on to Mark Fowler instead. They dated for several months, but she became clingy and tried emotional blackmail to stop him dumping her until Mark wised up and gave her the old heave-ho.

Della Alexander

Alexander

Arrived in the Square Mar 94 **Left** May 9

(Michelle Joseph)

Della (*far left and below*) was one half of *EastEnders'* first lesbian couple with Binnie Roberts, although she found it hard to face up to her sexuality and initially kept it secret, tacitly encouraging Steve Elliott. They set up a hairdressing salon together – Kool for Kutz – but it wasn't until Steve found her in bed with Binnie that he got the message and flounced off. Della eventually came out by snogging Binnie in the middle of Bridge Street, which really gave the gossips something to talk about.

Binnie Roberts

Roberts

Arrived in the Square Jun 94 **Left** May 95

(Sophie Langham)

Unlike girlfriend Della, Binnie (*above, right*) was relaxed about being gay and tried to persuade Della to acknowledge their relationship. She finally gave her an ultimatum – come out or I'm off – sparking the infamous lesbian kiss. Binnie's job at the Vic made for a tense working atmosphere with simmering Steve, but they eventually came to an uneasy truce. Della and Binnie left in May 1995 to work in the sunnier and more liberal climate of Ibiza.

Richard Cole

Tricky Dicky

Arrived in the Square Jul 92 **Left** Jul 94

(Ian Reddington)

Market inspector Tricky Dicky, as he was known to everyone, was well-named: he was sly, underhand and ruthless, both in his business dealings (he had stitched up Sanjay and Gita) and with women. He was good-looking in an oily sort of way, but dropped his girlfriends once he'd got another notch on his bedpost. Rachel Kominsky and Bianca Jackson both got the treatment, although Kathy Beale lasted a little longer. Richard also chased after Cindy Beale, who didn't sleep with him, even though he declared her baby to be his. Unsurprisingly, given that he'd messed with his mum and his wife, there was no love lost between Ian Beale and Tricky Dicky, and when Ian found out that Richard had done a runner with £40,000 of a former colleague's cash he threatened to dish the dirt. Richard took the hint and left the same day.

Tavernier
Jules

Arrived in the Square Jul 90 **Left** Dec 97
(Tommy Eytle)

With his snowy beard, granny (or should that be grandpa?) glasses and felt hat, elderly Jules Tavernier – Celestine's father – revelled in his mildly eccentric reputation. He loved to talk about the old days in Trinidad and had always been a bit of a ladykiller, which was confirmed when Gidea, his granddaughter from an affair he had in his 20's, turned up looking for him. Even in his 70's, Jules was still chasing women. He flirted naughtily with Dot and Ethel, and 'girlfriends' Nellie and Blossom *(above)* moved into his flat at different times. Perhaps Jules was losing his touch, though: Nellie made him sleep on the sofa, giving him a bad back, and all he and Blossom got up to in bed was board games! He also enjoyed playing chess with Felix Kawalski, who was furious when Jules keeled over asleep in the middle of an important tournament, scattering the pieces.

Besides her family, the other big love of Etta's life was teaching. However, when she was appointed acting head of Walford Primary School, husband Celestine couldn't handle her higher status and earning power, which caused big rows. Already feeling undermined as a man, he became even more entrenched when Etta told him she wanted to be sterilised. Etta went ahead anyway, only to discover she was pregnant, but when tests showed the baby had sickle-cell anaemia she had a termination. It was a traumatic time but the couple eventually emerged from it stronger and closer, and Celestine was genuinely happy for her when she got a permanent headteacher's job.

Etta&Celestine
Tavernier

Arrived in the Square Jul 90
Left Mar 94
(Jacqui Gordon-Lawrence)

Arrived in the Square Jul 90
Left Jul 93
(Leroy Golding)

Celestine couldn't handle Etta's higher status and earning power

Celestine was a devout church-goer and all-round model citizen who, having pulled himself up by his boot straps, tended to be unbending with his children, expecting them to show similar dedication. He worked for the DSS, which put him in an awkward position when he discovered that Arthur Fowler was working and signing on, although not as awkward a position as when he was propositioned by a young girl from church who he'd been helping with Bible studies. It was a testing time for Celestine, who was feeling displaced by his wife Etta's professional success, but the couple surmounted their personal difficulties and eventually moved away when Celestine got a new job in Norwich.

Ian developed
an obsession
and tried to
kiss her

Tavernier Hattie

Arrived in the Square Jul 90 **Left** Dec 93

(Michelle Gayle)

Tavernier Lloyd

Arrived in the Square Jul 90 **Left** Jun 92

(Garey Bridges)

Lloyd, Hattie's twin, had sickle-cell anaemia, an inherited condition, which made him easily tired. After secretly taking on a paper round he collapsed and was rushed to hospital, underlining the seriousness of his condition. His family tended to be overprotective of him and he rebelled by turning to petty crime, getting caught in a stolen car, which, to Celestine's shame, earned him a suspended sentence.

Hattie was an intelligent girl with a promising future, so her parents were horrified when she left school at 16 and became a waitress at The Meal Machine. Employer Ian Beale soon promoted her to his secretary and they worked well together – so well that Ian developed an obsession and tried to kiss her, earning himself a knee in the groin. Hattie started dating Steve Elliott, an old school friend, but she was always the more committed one, and once caught him with another girl. Despite this she proposed to him, but the wedding never happened: Steve did a bunk and a heartbroken Hattie was left alone and pregnant. After much soul-searching she decided to keep the baby, but it wasn't to be, and two days later she had a miscarriage.

Beefy Clyde, the Taverniers' eldest, worked at the Vic, although it wasn't long before the Mitchell bruvs tried to exploit him in the boxing ring. Their scam backfired when an overfaced Clyde nevertheless managed to win his big fight, but his local hero status was quickly tarnished after Nick Cotton framed him for Eddie Royle's murder. Single parent Clyde and his son Kofi went on the run with girlfriend Michelle Fowler and her daughter, Vicki (*all pictured right*), but only got as far as Portsmouth before Clyde was arrested and charged. He was imprisoned but released three months later after Nick confessed. Clyde and Michelle split when he found her in bed with student Jack; he subsequently fell for second cousin Gidea and they went off to Trinidad together.

Tavernier
Clyde

Arrived in the Square Jul 90
Left Jul 93
(Steven Woodcock)

Mandy Salter

Arrived in the Square Mar 92 **Left** Jan 94

(Nicola Stapleton)

You wanted to feel sorry for homeless waif Mandy but her deviousness made it hard to even like her. Having been dumped by her mum, she drifted round the Square, frequently sleeping rough or kipping with whoever would put her up, until she met and fell in love with Aidan. They moved from squat to squat in a destructive downward spiral – Mandy even tried clipping to make money. It almost ended in tragedy for Aidan and, incidentally, proved fatal for Roly the dog, who got run over when kiss-of-death Mandy took him for a walk.

She drifted round the Square, frequently sleeping rough

Nadia Borovac

Arrived in the Square June 93 **Left** Aug

(Anna Barkan)

Nadia was a Romanian refugee who met Phil Mitchell in a Portsmouth bar and persuaded him to marry her to stop her being deported. Rashly, Phil agreed, thinking he'd never see Nadia again, only to have her turn up on his doorstep four months later demanding he act like a proper husband. A drunk Phil did his conjugal duty once, causing all sorts of trouble with Kathy. Grant saw Nadia off but she still managed to con Phil out of a grand before she gave him a divorce.

Brosnan
Aidan

Arrived in the Square Jan 93 **Left** Dec 93

(Sean Maguire)

Aidan was a naive Irish lad who came to Walford to play football (Walford Town apparently being a Mecca for young footie talent). He initially lodged at the Fowlers' and, after a knee injury shattered his dreams of a sporting career, turned to drink and drugs (Ecstasy), egged on by Mandy and Ricky. Homeless and broke, Aidan became chronically depressed after falling out with his family and tried to commit suicide by jumping off a tower block. Mandy talked him out of it, but he wanted no more to do with her and returned to Ireland alone.

Christine Hewitt

Arrived in the Square Feb 92 **Left** Oct 93

(Elizabeth Power)

Arthur chose Pauline and Christine presumably went back to gin and daytime television

Rachel Kominski

Arrived in the Square Mar 91 **Left** Mar 93

(Jacquetta May)

Lonely Christine Hewitt had a certain pathos, sitting in all afternoon drinking. However, she soon found more pleasurable ways to occupy her time by chatting up Arthur Fowler, who was doing her garden. She inveigled her way into his life, offering her services as a gardening assistant and looking after him while Pauline was away in New Zealand. He turned her down the first time she made a pass and they didn't actually sleep together until Christmas Day 1992. After that she became bolder, getting a job at the bistro to be closer to him and making more demands, before issuing him with an ultimatum. Arthur chose Pauline, and Christine presumably went back to gin and daytime television.

Lecturer Rachel was accorded a certain amount of mistrust in Walford where young, professional, middle-class women with posh accents were thin on the ground. Michelle Fowler became her lodger and friend, a relationship that helped her re-evaluate her life. They had a sticky start – Michelle was unused to the dinner-party set – but Rachel saw her potential and encouraged her to apply for college, which she did. Through Michelle, Rachel met Mark, with whom she had an on-off relationship for six months. When Rachel's courses were dropped, she was reduced to working in the café and then ran a bric-a-brac stall, a decline in taste that was reflected in her love life when she slept with Tricky Dicky. How the mighty are fallen!

Willmott-Brown
James

Arrived in the Square Mar 86 **Left** Feb 92

(William Boyde)

Boo! Hiss! James Willmott-Brown was as much a rotter as Nick Cotton, more so probably because he dressed so nicely and had lovely blonde hair. He owned the Dagmar wine bar where Kathy Beale worked, and where he famously raped her one night. He was eventually jailed for three years, and on release came straight back to find Kathy, having convinced himself that she loved him. Kathy – with Pete in attendance – put him straight about this once and for all and he left, only to end up back inside for raping another woman.

Disa O'Brien

Arrived in the Square Mar 90
Left Feb 91

(Jan Graveson)

Homeless teenager Disa *(below, right)* was a former street pal of Diane Butcher's who turned up in Walford on Christmas Day 1990 and left her newborn baby on Diane's doorstep. Diane and Dot helped the girl to bond with her baby, but then her stepfather Ken – who had raped Disa, fathering baby Jasmine – snatched the child. Dot's initiative caught him and when the truth about his abuse came out, Disa's mum, Sandra, dumped him and took runaway Disa and little Jasmine in.

Eddie Royle

Arrived in the Square Jul 90 **Died** Sep 91

(Michael Melia)

Ex-copper Eddie was landlord of the Vic, although he's best remembered for the manner of his passing than for his talent for pulling pints. A solitary man, he had a brief fling with Kathy Beale and later proposed to his Irish girlfriend, Eibhlin. The marriage never took place because Eddie was found stabbed to death in the Square. Grant, who had beaten him half to death for making a pass at Sharon, was originally top of a long list of suspects and 'Who Killed Eddie Royle?' remained the question on people's lips for many months until culprit Nick Cotton confessed, after being put on the spot by Dot.

Cooper
Julie

Arrived in the Square Jun 89 **Left** Mar 90

(Louise Plowright)

Ludlow
Donna

Arrived in the Square Aug 87
Died Apr 89

(Matilda Ziegler)

A proficient liar and cheat

Pinched-faced Donna was the daughter Kathy Beale gave away for adoption at 15, the result of a rape, but when she tried to weasel her way into Kathy's affections, Kathy just didn't want to know. Donna was a proficient liar and cheat and, after becoming hooked on heroin, turned to blackmail and prostitution and became truly evil. Rod (*above, left*), with whom she lived in the squat for a while, couldn't handle her drug addiction and left, and Dot took her under her wing, but even her mother hen act couldn't save self-destructive Donna. She died a grim death choking on her own vomit after a heroin overdose. Dot, Rod and Kathy all felt guilty, but the truth was Donna's fate seemed to have been sealed from the moment of her disastrous conception.

Julie's mane of tousled, bleached, backcombed locks always seemed more suited to an escort girl than a senior stylist. Unsurprisingly, when she opened her hairdresser's on Turpin Road, Dot and Ethel, misled by the 'personal service' advertised on her flier, thought it was a brothel. Julie certainly had an appetite for men, going to bed with Paul Priestly, Laurie Bates and Grant Mitchell, but she was sussed enough to realise that Grant and Phil were wooing her for her flat, and made a good profit out of them.

Although they looked contented enough the relationship was a sham

The Karims
Ashraf, Sufia, Shireen & Sohail

Arrived in the Square Ashraf: Jul 87; Sufia, Shireen & Sohail: Mar 88 **Left** Jun 90

Ashraf (Aftab Sachak), Sufia (Rani Singh), Shireen (Nisha Kapur), Sohail (Ronnie Jhutti)

Ashraf and Sufia Karim (*right*) owned and ran the First 'til Last and had two teenage children, Shireen and Sohail (*above*). The Karims' was an arranged marriage and although they looked contented enough, the relationship was a sham. Handsome Ashraf kept a mistress, Stella, and Sufia, who knew about her, was deeply hurt by this. At one point she took a stand and threatened to leave him, but stayed when Ashraf told her it was all finished, unaware that he was carrying on as before. A heavy-handed Ashraf clamped down on Shireen's innocent friendship with Ricky and even took her to Dr Legg, asking him to prove she was still a virgin (he wouldn't). In a bid to keep Shireen away from boys he sent her to a girls' boarding school, and when that failed (she ran away), the Karims decided to arrange a marriage for her. Shireen was horrified until she met her intended, Jabbar (*below, left*) and found herself genuinely attracted to him. The wedding was cancelled when Jabbar's family found out about Ashraf's mistress, but the two mothers later met secretly to plot how to keep the engagement going, much to Shireen's delight. Whether it took place we'll never know, as the Karims moved to Bristol.

Paul Priestly

Arrived in the Square Apr 89 **Left** Mar 90

(Mark Thrippleton)

Hunky Paul was a labourer and odd-job man who soon set 16-year-old Diane Butcher's heart fluttering when he lodged at the Vic. They started going out but it wasn't long before Julie 'The Hair' Cooper got her claws into him, realising she'd get a cheaper quote for her renovations plus additional benefits. When Paul twigged this he went back to a pathetically grateful Diane, until she got too heavy for him and he bolted home to Leeds.

Trevor Short

Arrived in the Square Jun 89 **Left** Mar 90

(Phil McDermott)

Trevor was Paul Priestly's dopey sidekick, but he bodged jobs so often you wondered why Paul kept him on. Among others, his list of disasters included striking a water main, flooding the market and making the Karims' ceiling collapse. He was a bit slow (to be kind) and happy to be bossed around by landlady Mo Butcher, but he never had a girlfriend, despite his crushes on Diane Butcher and Shireen Karim.

Rod Norman

Arrived in the Square Jul 87 **Left** Feb 90

(Christopher McHallem)

In his battered leather jacket and dusty black clothes, 'Rod the Roadie' was a modern-day hobo. He dossed in squats and never settled anywhere for long, although he did return to Albert Square several times. Actually, Rod was an OK guy, though he was a sucker for female hopeless cases. He tried (unsuccessfully) to get Punk Mary off pills and prostitution and Donna off heroin, although he did succeed in weaning Hazel off abusive boyfriend Nick Cotton before leaving again, this time to hit the hippy trail in India.

Duncan Boyd

Arrived in the Square Oct 87 **Left** Jul 89

(David Gillespie)

Wimpy curate Duncan wasn't Sharon Watts' usual choice of bloke – she was more used to being chased than being chaste – but after all Den and Angie's fighting she yearned for a quiet life. So what if it came with a dog collar? They got engaged, but when Duncan told her he'd been offered a parish in leafy Wiltshire and wanted to get married immediately, Sharon decided that she wasn't cut out for tea at the vicarage and sensibly broke it off.

Carmel Jackson

Arrived in the Square Jun 86 **Left** Aug 89

(Judith Jacob)

Carmel was a health visitor who was forever getting dumped on. Unreliable brother Darren foisted himself and his kids on her when he helped move her into the Square, and later landed her with them after he did a runner. But the biggest disaster of all was Carmel's marriage to seemingly nice Matthew Jackson, who turned out to be violent. She suffered it, trying to help him change, but after six months of abuse finally walked out while she still could.

Matthew Jackson

Arrived in the Square May 88 **Left** Jul 89

(Steven Hartley)

Matthew's Jekyll-and-Hyde personality didn't show up until the day he married Carmel. Until then, the good-looking professional had been Mr Wonderful – hell, he was even OK about taking on delinquent Junior. Because of this, the emergence of his violent side was truly shocking, and all the more so because he was always so tearful and contrite afterwards. However, it was Matthew himself who finally ended up in hospital when Junior, defending Carmel, stabbed him. Even after this Matthew refused to get professional help, so Carmel wisely left him.

Ali was a happy-go-lucky sort, unlike his highly strung wife Sue

Sue & Ali Usman

Arrived in the Square Feb 85
Left Oct 89
(Nejdet Salih)

Arrived in the Square Feb 85 **Left** May 89
(Sandy Ratcliff)

Ali was a Turkish Cypriot who ran the café with his wife, Sue, as well as a minicab business with his brother, Mehmet (remember Ozcabs?). Ali and Mehmet were both compulsive gamblers and prepared to stake their businesses in a poker game. The first time Ali did this he won; when Mehmet did it he lost everything and his wife Guizin and three children landed on Ali and Sue's doorstep. Ali was a happy-go-lucky sort, unlike his highly strung wife, Sue, who never recovered from losing their first son, Hassan, to cot death. She became obsessed with the idea of having another child, imagining a phantom pregnancy and even asking Michelle if she could adopt Vicki. Three stormy years after Hassan's death Sue fell pregnant for real and gave birth to little Ali, but after a furious bust up with her husband (who had slept with prostitute Donna Ludlow), Sue left taking their son with her. Ali found them at Hassan's grave and snatched the baby back, which was the final straw for Sue's parlous emotional state. She was taken to a mental hospital and never released. Left alone, Ali's gambling proved his downfall and, having lost the café to Ian Beale and been evicted from his flat, he went back to Cyprus.

Colin Russell

Arrived in the Square Aug 86 **Left** Feb 89

(Michael Cashman)

Yuppy graphic designer Colin was gay. He kept this secret for some time until Dot, standing in for cleaning lady Pauline, worked out that he shared his bed with boyfriend Barry and went into panic mode. Colin and Barry were *EastEnders'* first gay couple and their first screen kiss generated an extraordinary amount of hoo-haa. After Barry, Colin had a short-lived relationship with Guido, but by then he had developed a mystery illness that at first looked as if it might be Aids. It actually turned out to be MS, and a few months later he left to be looked after by his brother in Bristol.

Barry Clark

Arrived in the Square Nov 86 **Left** Feb 89

(Gary Hailes)

Cockney barrowboy Barry (*far right*) was an unlikely choice of partner for middle-class Colin. Given the age difference – Barry was considerably younger – and the fact that Colin was always baling him out of trouble (Barry was influenced by Nick Cotton), Colin's role was almost paternal. Perhaps that was because Barry, who was out to everyone else, had never told his father – and when he did, his dad took the news badly. Barry tried to go straight to appease his father after he and Colin split, but he was never very successful at it.

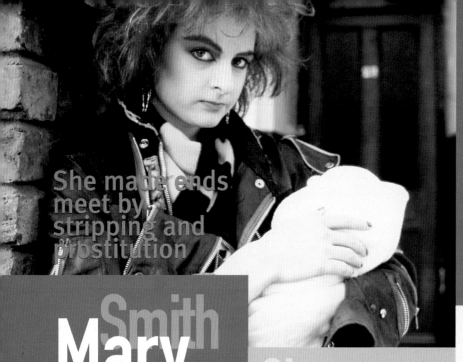

She made ends meet by stripping and prostitution

arren, who initially lived with sister Carmel, had two children: Junior, who was always getting into trouble, and toddler Aisha. He was a wideboy who got involved in various dodgy scams, including holding a 'cultural evening' in the community centre, which was a front for a porn film and stripper (Dot wandered in on it and fainted). He was forced to vacate the Square hurriedly after HP men repossessed a mobile disco he'd sold to Barry and Ian, and somehow he forgot to come back for his kids.

Smith
Mary

Arrived in the Square Mar 85
Died May 88

(Linda Davidson)

Punk Mary had scary hair and even scarier makeup. A single mum – she had an illegitimate daughter, Annie – she made ends meet by stripping and prostitution. Both Andy O'Brien and Rod Norman tried to help Mary sort herself out, but she rapidly reverted to type, this time leaving the toddler 'home alone' which nearly ended in tragedy. Mary's parents took Annie away for her own safety, which temporarily brought Mary to her senses, but even after Annie was returned to her, Mary lapsed again, finally shooting through Walford and heading for a life of who knows what.

Clements
Tom

Arrived in the Square Sept 86
Died Apr 88

(Donald Tandy)

Tom was an allotment rival of Arthur Fowler's who was always battling with him over the length of his leeks or the size of his marrows. He had a thing for Dot and did a council house swap with her, but it didn't sweeten her enough to consent to marry him when he proposed. He was a potman at the Vic and died on the job (so to speak), ignominiously popping his clogs in the gents from a heart attack.

Roberts
Darren

Arrived in the Square Jul 87 **Left** Jul 88

(Gary MacDonald)

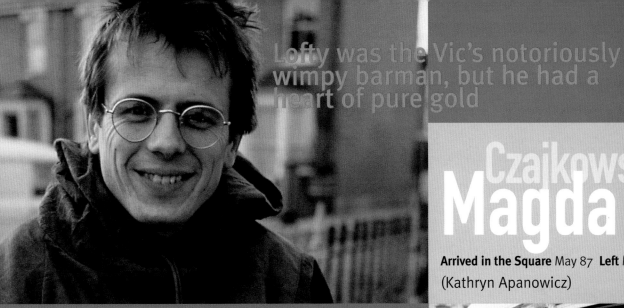

Lofty was the Vic's notoriously wimpy barman, but he had a heart of pure gold

Czajkowski
Magda

Arrived in the Square May 87 **Left** Mar 88

(Kathryn Apanowicz)

'Lofty' Holloway

Arrived in the Square Feb 85 **Left** Apr 88

(Tom Watt)

Bumbling, asthmatic Lofty (real name George) was the Vic's notoriously wimpy barman, but he had a heart of pure gold. This was sorely abused by Michelle Fowler, who agreed to marry him to get a father for Vicki, but when the time came she hesitated outside the church and turned away... (though she did marry him later). Chelle also aborted Lofty's much-longed-for baby without telling him, which broke the poor lad: he called her a murderer, cleared out of their flat and eventually left the Square – to work in a children's home.

Half-Polish, half-Yorkshire 'Mags', as she was always known, was a caterer for the Vic who soon found herself making more than lasagne with Den Watts. When Den came on all heavy Mags backed off and started seeing Wicksy instead. They moved in together and Mags thought it was the Real Thing at last, but Wicksy, whose only real commitment was to his hair gel, soon grew bored, and when Mags wanted to make the arrangement more permanent he decided her hot dinners weren't worth the hassle, and they parted.

The original and – well, let's just say he set the standard for every other sexy villain Walford's produced since *EastEnders* began. Den, of course, was the first landlord of the Vic, with his wife Angie as First Lady and adopted daughter Sharon as the Princess (Den's affectionate name for her). Den and Angie's volatile and destructive marriage was played out in full view of the Vic's regulars: it was clear from the off that he had a mistress (Jan) and, however often he promised the affair was over, it never was. Only when Angie told him she had months to live did Den really commit to her (taking her on a second honeymoon to Venice), but when he found out what a whopper she'd told him he served up divorce papers with a snarl on Christmas Day. Jan's attempt to take Angie's place at the Vic didn't last long. She couldn't stand Den's flirting with other women. Then he took up with caterer Mags Czaikowski, but she didn't like being bossed around and left him too. Womaniser Den's most famous infidelity was with schoolgirl Michelle *(above, right)*, Sharon's best mate, a one-off that produced baby Vicki. He didn't love Chelle but he did love Vicki and made sure she was provided for – which was just as well. Den's exorbitant divorce from Angie in 1987 put him in hock to The Firm, a local protection racket, who appointed him manager of Strokes Wine Bar

under the viperous Joanne, and then decided he was a liability when he got the Dagmar torched to avenge Kathy. He was told to take the rap and go down for it, but the Firm thought he was grassing them up from inside (he wasn't) and had him shot and disposed of – in the dank depths of Walford Canal. It wasn't a glorious life, but it was an utterly compelling one.

He set the standard for every other sexy villain Walford's produced

Angie's solution was to embrace her own faithful companion, the bottle

Den&Angie

Arrived in the Square Feb 85
Died Feb 89

(Leslie Grantham)

Arrived in the Square Feb 85
Left May 88

(Anita Dobson)

For a couple that argued so passionately, Den and Angie didn't do much making up the traditional way. Their sex life was pretty non-existent, and had been for years, which explains why Den had so many affairs and why Sharon was adopted. Angie's solution was to embrace her own faithful companion, the bottle, though she had liaisons too (Tony Carpenter, Andy O'Brien), purely to provoke a reaction from Den, who she loved above everything. Angie made out that she was alright, painting on a front, dressing to kill, screeching raucously with the girls,

but inside she was a mess. When she discovered Den was living with Jan she took an overdose and was lucky to be found in time. Later, in desperation, she made up a story about her imminent demise which blew up in her face when Den found out the truth and divorced her. Angie did try and get her act together: she found a place to live, got a new job (at the Dagmar), and went on the wagon. It wasn't enough to win Den back as a husband, but he did take her back as a business partner, which she found impossible to handle and made her start drinking again. As a result Angie was rushed to

hospital with kidney failure, though even then she took advantage of her straitened circumstances to propose to Den from her hospital bed (he turned her down). When she was discharged she went to Spain to recuperate with friends Sonny and Ree and started an affair with Sonny. On her return, she walked out of Walford and Den's life for good to live with Sonny, although this didn't work out either and Angie moved to Florida. She soon nabbed a nameless rich bloke and is presumably bitching happily by a pool somewhere with a (hopefully) non-alcoholic cocktail close to hand.

The Carpenters

The Carpenters

Trinidadian Tony was separated from his wife, Hannah, and lived with son Kelvin at number 3 Albert Square. Tony, a builder, was renovating the house and did handyman jobs to bring in money. Angie Watts, who was trying to make Den jealous, found Tony very handy indeed, but finished their brief affair when it had served its purpose. Tony was deeply hurt, but Hannah's arrival took his mind off it and when he found out that her new man was beating her and daughter Cassie, Tony squared up to him. For a while the couple tried to make another go of it, but Tony was never good enough for Hannah and she constantly harangued him. Despite having been happy for Tony to hit her abusive boyfriend, Hannah was not pleased when he thumped Mehmet Osman for making a pass at her and she stalked off to stay with her sister. A depressed Tony left soon after and returned to Trinidad. While all this was going on, Kelvin was carving his way through a string of girls, including

Tony was never good enough for Hannah

Tony, Hannah, Cassie & Kelvin

Arrived in the Square
Feb 85 **Left** May 87

(Oscar James)

Arrived in the Square
Jun 85 **Left** Feb 87

(Sally Sagoe)

Arrived in the Square
Nov 85 **Left** Dec 86

(Delanie Forbes)

Arrived in the Square
Feb 85 **Left** Sep 87

(Paul Medford)

Michelle, Sharon and Carmel. Carmel even moved in with him but soon got fed up with her immature toyboy (Kelvin was still only 16!) and left. Kelvin was bright and showed plenty of initiative when it suited him, starting a knitting business with Ian and Lofty ('Loftelian') and a band ('The Banned') with Ian, Sharon and others. He passed his A levels and went to university, and with sister Cassie at boarding school, that was the last we saw of the Carpenters.

Debbie Watkins

Arrived in the Square Mar 85 **Left** May 87

(Shirley Cheriton)

Jan Hammond

Arrived in the Square Jan 86 **Left** May 87

(Jane How)

Angie's frequent digs about Jan, Den's long-standing mistress, gave her quite a build up, but when she finally strolled into the Vic, Angie – and everyone else – was taken aback by the sophisticated PR woman. Over the next few months the two women battled it out, Jan giving Den ultimatums and Angie using dirty tricks, pretending she was dying. Jan got her feet behind the bar eventually, but proved to be entirely unsuited for pub life and when she and Den rowed, Angie-style, Jan went right off him and opted for boyfriend-in-the-background, Dario O'Brien, instead.

Neat blonde Debbie and Andy, her on-off fiancé, had a rocky relationship from the word go. She wanted to make money; he wanted to settle down, a situation complicated by the fact that she was also being wooed by lovestruck policeman Roy Quick. She plumped for Andy but he was killed in a tragic road accident. Debs was almost assaulted by the Walford Attacker and met another policeman, DI Terry Rich, who was only too happy to take down her particulars on a regular basis.

Jan got her feet behind the bar eventually but proved to be entirely unsuited for pub life

Naima & Saeed

Jeffery

Naima

Arrived in the Square Feb 85
Left Nov 87

(Shreela Ghosh)

Saeed

Arrived in the Square Feb 85
Left Dec 85

(Andrew Johnson)

Like the Karims after them, the Jefferys ran the shop and had an arranged marriage. At first they didn't sleep together and Saeed took out his frustrations making obscene phone calls, visiting prostitutes and going to the strip club where Mary Smith worked. Naima discovered this after their marital *détente* and divorced him. She made a determined attempt to embrace western culture (dating Wicksy!), but her family persisted in sending her cousins to marry and although the first, Rezaul, was an arrogant pig, the second one, Farrukh, was a sweetie, so she took the plunge again.

Her family persisted in sending her cousins to marry

Andy O'Brien

Arrived in the Square Mar 85 **Died** Aug 86

(Ross Davidson)

Male nurse Andy had always shown concern for the welfare of others, making a fuss of a small boy with chronic eczema, teaching illiterate punk Mary to read, and keeping Angie sexually satisfied after Den dumped her (more of an ordeal than a good deed), but his final act of heroism cost him his own life. On his way to work, he ran out in front of a lorry to save a child and was mown down himself. Altruistic to the end, his organ-donor card ensured someone got his kidneys. What a guy.

Roly

Roly

Willy

Willy

Roly, a fluffy white standard poodle, was essentially the Vic's dog. He was in *EastEnders* for seven years and originally belonged to Den and Angie, before being passed on to Pat and Frank, then Mo Butcher, then, finally, Sharon and Grant. Roly led an eventful and sometimes dangerous life, but then it came with the territory. He nearly died from eating rat poison put down by Debs; he was thrown out by hard-hearted Pat; he was injured in a car crash caused by a drunk Pete Beale and he was nearly burned alive (along with Sharon) when Grant had the Vic torched for the insurance money. After cheating death so many times, the end came when useless Mandy Salter took him for a walk and let him get run over. Still, he had a good innings, as they say.

Willy, Ethel's pug, went everywhere with her, which sometimes caused problems. While he was tolerated in the Vic, Ethel's attempts to sneak him on an OAP's holiday to Clacton in her holdall almost backfired on her – though fortunately, the B&B owner, a dog-lover too, relented. Willy was obviously a sensitive little soul: Ethel was convinced that he'd been upset by Dr Legg's careless remarks about dog mess in the Square to the extent that he couldn't perform at all. Luckily, both Willy's constipation and the dog fouling issue were resolved with satisfaction on both sides. Willy was eventually put down in 1992 after becoming ill. The Vic regulars clubbed together to buy her a new dog, but Ethel wouldn't accept, saying Willy was irreplaceable. He continues to snuffle by her side in spirit.

Roly led an eventful and sometimes dangerous life

Frieda

Frieda was purchased in a greyhound-racing scam dreamed up by Nigel and Grant in 1993 and was bought to be a ringer for another greyhound they had, Delilah. Unfortunately, the deception was spotted so they couldn't race either of them, but Grant kept Frieda on as a family pet and was frequently seen walking her round the Square with her little rug on. In October 1995 she got pregnant by Wellard and her puppies were stillborn. Robbie was devastated, and even Grant was upset, although being

Wellard

Wellard was a mangy German Shepherd who Robbie discovered hanging around the Square and eventually adopted after Carol caved in. He turned out not to be a stray at all and was reclaimed by his owner, Mr Hammond, but promptly found his way back to Robbie after being mistreated. Robbie and Alan confronted Hammond, who let him keep Wellard. Robbie has always been protective of him and when his new girlfriend, Tina (who was allergic to Wellard) made him choose between her and the dog, he chose Wellard. Wellard has at least had a better time with the opposite sex: he mated with Grant's greyhound, Frieda. Wellard still lives at the Jackson house with Sonia, Robbie and Grandpa Jim, but appears to be keeping a very low profile these days.

Grant, he kept his grief buried deep in his manly chest. Not only was Frieda unable to race, but the one time Grant himself entered a race (ironically against portly Nigel), it was Frieda who prevented him from winning by tripping him up before the finish. Since Grant left for sunnier climes, Frieda has been sent up to Edinburgh to live with Nigel, a fitting reward for her noble intervention.

Gone but not forgotten

Starsky and Hutch, Debbie and Andy's kittens; Crush the snake, who belonged to Mehmet's kids and caused chaos in the café; Mandoo, Auntie Nellie's cat, found dead under Joe Wicks's bed; and Bella, Rosa's much-disputed cat, who was taken in by Pauline (and re-christened Tigger).

index of entries